# NIKLAS LUHMANN

*Niklas Luhmann* offers an accessible introduction to one of the most important sociologists of our time. It presents the key concepts within Luhmann's multifaceted theory of modern society, and compares them with the work of other key social theorists such as Jürgen Habermas, Michel Foucault and Zygmunt Bauman.

The book pays particular attention to introducing and discussing Luhmann's original sociological systems theory. It presents a thorough investigation into the different phases of his oeuvre, through which both the shifting emphases as well as the continuities in his thinking are shown. The primary focus of this text is Luhmann's theory of modern society as being differentiated into a plethora of 'function systems' – such as politics, law and economy – which operate according to their own distinct logics and which cannot interfere with one another. For Luhmann, this functional differentiation works as a bulwark against totalitarian rule, and as such is a key foundation of modern democracy. Furthermore, the book critically examines the implications of this functional differentiation for inclusion and exclusion dynamics, as well as for the understanding of power and politics.

This is a key text for both undergraduate and postgraduate students of areas including contemporary social theory, political sociology and sociology.

**Christian Borch** is an Associate Professor at the Department of Management, Politics and Philosophy, Copenhagen Business School, Denmark. His research interests include sociological systems theory, power, sociology of crowds and architecture.

D1518175

## KEY SOCIOLOGISTS
Edited by PETER HAMILTON

This classic series provides students with concise and readable introductions to the work, life and influence of the great sociological thinkers. With individual volumes covering individual thinkers, from Emile Durkheim to Pierre Bourdieu, each author takes a distinct line, assessing the impact of these major figures on the discipline as well as the contemporary relevance of their work. These pocket-sized introductions will be ideal for both undergraduates and pre-university students alike, as well as for anyone with an interest in the thinkers who have shaped our time.

Series titles include:

**EMILE DURKHEIM**
*Ken Thompson*

**THE FRANKFURT SCHOOL AND ITS CRITICS**
*Tom Bottomore*

**GEORG SIMMEL**
*David Frisby*

**MARX AND MARXISM**
*Peter Worsley*

**MAX WEBER**
*Frank Parkin*

**MICHEL FOUCAULT**
*Barry Smart*

**PIERRE BOURDIEU**
*Richard Jenkins*

**SIGMUND FREUD**
*Robert Bocock*

**ZYGMUNT BAUMAN**
*Tony Blackshaw*

**AUGUSTE COMTE**
*Mike Gane*

**ERVING GOFFMAN**
*Greg Smith*

**JEAN BAUDRILLARD**
*William Pawlett*

**NIKLAS LUHMANN**
*Christian Borch*

# NIKLAS LUHMANN

CHRISTIAN BORCH

Routledge
Taylor & Francis Group

LONDON AND NEW YORK

First published 2011
by Routledge
2 Park Square, Milton Park, Abingdon, Oxon OX14 4RN

Simultaneously published in the USA and Canada
by Routledge
711 Third Avenue, New York, NY 10017

*Routledge is an imprint of the Taylor & Francis Group, an informa business*

*British Library Cataloguing in Publication Data*
A catalogue record for this book is available from the British
Library

*Library of Congress Cataloging in Publication Data*
Borch, Christian.
Niklas Luhmann : in defence of modernity/Christian Borch.
    p. cm.—(Key sociologists)
  Includes bibliographical references and index.
  ISBN-10: 0-415-49093-6 (cloth: alk.paper)
  [etc.]
  1. Luhmann, Niklas, 1927–1998.   2. System theory.
  3. Social structure.   I. Title.
  HM479.L84B67 2011
  301.092—dc22
                                           2010039921

ISBN: 978-0-415-49093-1 (hbk)
ISBN: 978-0-415-49094-8 (pbk)
ISBN: 978-0-203-88052-4 (ebk)

Typeset in Bembo
by RefineCatch Limited, Bungay, Suffolk
Printed and bound in Great Britain by
TJ International Ltd, Padstow, Cornwall

For Susanne

# Contents

# Illustrations

# Acknowledgements

The author would like to thank the following for permission to reprint material of his previously published work:

*Distinktion Scandinavian Journal of Social Theory* for kind permission to reprint material from Christian Borch (2000) 'Former, der kommer i form – om Luhmann og Spencer-Brown', *Distinktion* 1: 105–22.

Sage Publications Ltd for kind permission to reprint material from Christian Borch (2005) 'Systemic Power: Luhmann, Foucault, and Analytics of Power', *Acta Sociologica* 48(2): 155–67.

Samfundslitteratur for kind permission to reprint material from Christian Borch (2006) 'Niklas Luhmann: Magt som medium', pp. 385–407 in Carsten Bagge Laustsen and Jesper Myrup (eds) *Magtens tænkere: Politisk filosofi fra Machiavelli til Honneth*. Frederiksberg: Roskilde Universitetsforlag.

# 1

# Introduction

## A THEORY OF SOCIETY

Is it possible to grasp the complexity of the entire social world? How to account for phenomena ranging from the politics of climate change to the ways we address our beloved ones? Is it feasible within one single sociological framework to conceive of anything from modern science and economy to exclusion patterns in Brazilian *favelas*, and from legal decisions to the way artists communicate? While many would find such a challenge too big, the German sociologist Niklas Luhmann did not find it insurmountable. He developed an exceptionally sophisticated theory of society which was based on a simple severance, namely the distinction between a system and its environment. On the basis of this fundamental separation he set out to seize the complexity of the world, a venture he pursued in around 75 books and 500 articles.

Luhmann worked as a sociologist at Bielefeld University, Germany, where he was appointed professor in 1969 when the university had just been established. With a population today of around 330,000 people and located some 400 kilometres west of Berlin, Bielefeld does not occupy a central place in the German social and political landscape. Yet ever since its inauguration the city's university has created a very stimulating environment for sociological thought, which has attracted a number of prominent sociologists. For example, Nobert Elias was visiting professor at the university's sociological faculty for several years. Likewise, Karin Knorr Cetina was professor at Bielefeld University for almost two decades. It was within this intellectually inspiring environment that Luhmann developed his grand sociological project.

In a retrospective comment Luhmann has remarked that, when he came to Bielefeld University in 1969, he was asked to assign a title to his research project. 'My project was entitled, at that time and subsequently: theory of society; term: 30 years; costs: none' (1997a: 11). For Luhmann, a theory of society refers to a sociological theory which is able to account for all societal phenomena. It was to this great task that de devoted his academic career. Luhmann's emphasis on theory is not fortuitous, but rather an effect of the main problem he identified in the discipline of sociology. As he put it in a programmatic text,

> Sociology is stuck in a theory crisis. Empirical research, though it has, on the whole, been successful in increasing knowledge, has not been able to produce *a unified theory for the discipline*. Being an empirical science, sociology cannot give up the claim that it checks its statements against data drawn from reality, no matter how old or new the bottles may be into which these data are poured. But it cannot use this principle of empirical scrutiny to account for the distinctiveness of its specific domain of research or its unity as a scientific discipline. Resignation about this is so widespread that no one even attempts such accounts any longer.
>
> (Luhmann 1995g: xlv, italics added)

Luhmann could not accept this resignation. He therefore put all his energy into revitalising the idea of a universal sociological theory, i.e. a theory which would allow sociology to arrive at a more precise description of modern society in all its dimensions. Needless to say, creating such a unifying theory must be a highly abstract enterprise, and Luhmann made no pretentions that it would be an easy journey. Also, following the quote above, Luhmann professed that this journey would not be loaded with empirical data. Very appositely, he therefore used the metaphor of the pilot sitting in his or her cockpit to illustrate the venture:

> Our flight must take place above the clouds, and we must reckon with a rather thick cloud cover. We must rely on our instruments. Occasionally, we may catch glimpses below of a land with roads, towns, rivers, and coastlines that remind us of something familiar, or glimpses of a larger stretch of landscape with the extinct volcanoes of Marxism. But no one should fall victim to the illusion that these few points of reference are sufficient to guide our flight.
>
> (1995g: l)

This siding with abstract theorising gives a first indication of Luhmann's distinctive position in social theory. He did not infuse himself in empirical work as did, for example, Michel Foucault who, rather than the pilot flying high in the sky, described his wok by way of the metaphor of the sperm whale that only surfaces occasionally (Foucault 2003: 4). To be sure, the strong belief in a unifying sociological theory is something that has been fiercely contested, from C. Wright Mills' critique of Talcott Parsons to Bruno Latour's critique of the canonised sociological tradition from Emile Durkheim to Pierre Bourdieu. Put differently, not only would many resign when confronted with the task of developing a universal theory; quite some sociologists would also deny its relevance. Luhmann disagreed with this and argued that sociology could only progress if provided with a new theoretical edifice.

One cannot expect a theory which claims to be able to understand all social phenomena to be easy to comprehend. The complexity of the social world will necessarily have to be mirrored in the theoretical corpus. This also applies to Luhmann's sociology. Yet in Luhmann's case, the complexity is not only a reflection of the variety of social phenomena he analysed (law, politics, science, art, love, economy, etc.). It is just as much a consequence of his specific approach. Thus, rather than merely reinterpreting classical sociological theories such as those put forward by Emile Durkheim, Max Weber and Talcott Parsons, Luhmann developed his theoretical framework on a multiplicity of resources from biology, philosophy, mathematics, cybernetics and so-called general systems theory. The interdisciplinary inclusion of this variety of inspirational sources, with which only few social scientists are familiar, has contributed to the highly difficult, if not outright inaccessible, character that many sociologists (rightly) think that Luhmann's work has. However, it was also on the basis of this interdisciplinary approach that Luhmann arrived at some of his most thought-provoking ideas which sought to radically reformulate the foundation of modern sociology. For example, Luhmann entirely rejected the notion of subjects. Instead of operating with a basic distinction between subjects and objects, Luhmann suggested his separation between system and environment and argued that humans are not part of society, but belong instead to its environment. This idea is provocative in itself, but it appears even more astonishing when Luhmann at the same time centred his systems theory on the notion of communication and argued that it is not humans or subjects that communicate, but communication itself!

The present book is an attempt to unravel some of the complexity of Luhmann's sociology. It aims to demonstrate that, even if Luhmann applied a vocabulary which at first sight appears rather foreign, one actually only needs to be acquainted with a few central notions in order to start seeing the social world in an entirely new way, namely the way it emerges when observed from the vantage point of sociological systems theory.

The book is structured as follows. In this introductory chapter I will begin with some brief biographical remarks on Luhmann, weaving into these biographical details some notes on his early theoretical work, and end with an overview of the various phases one can identify in his oeuvre. Chapter 2 deals with the fundamental architecture of Luhmann's systems theory, including his notion of social systems, how they are conceived to be operationally closed and autopoietically organised and how social systems are distinguished from but nevertheless intimately related to psychic systems. Chapter 3 discusses Luhmann's turn to so-called second-observation and explores the epistemological consequences of his work. Chapters 4, 5 and 6 investigate different aspects of Luhmann's general diagnosis of modernity, namely that modern society's most significant trait is its functionally differentiated nature. First, Chapter 4 presents the key elements in this diagnosis: how functionally differentiated systems are organised. On this basis, Chapter 5 deals with the implications of functional differentiation. This discussion revolves around the de-centring of modern society that the diagnosis of functional differentiation entails, just as the consequences of this de-centring for society's ability to handle ecological challenges and problems of risk are addressed. The chapter also discusses a possible new mode of societal differentiation that Luhmann identifies, namely that of inclusion/exclusion. Chapter 6 goes into detail with the political function system and also critically discusses Luhmann's conception of power. Common to chapters 4, 5 and 6 is the attempt to make explicit the normative agenda underpinning Luhmann's diagnosis of functional differentiation. I thus contend that, contrary to Luhmann's self-proclaimed non-normativity, his discussions of functional differentiation bear witness to a clear normative defence of modernity. At times this normative defence is very explicit, at other times it appears in disguise. Finally, in Chapter 7, I summarise what I see as Luhmann's main sociological achievements, as well as some of the main blind spots in his work.

I attempt in my approach to Luhmann to be loyal, but critical. Without being dogmatic, I will try to be faithful to Luhmann's main ideas and flesh out some of the highly stimulating and thought-provoking suggestions that his systems theory offers. But I will also engage critically with his perspective and highlight what I consider controversial or problematic propositions. The critical reflections will appear throughout the book, but will be unfolded especially in the final chapters. In order to see the strengths and weaknesses of Luhmann's theory, I will relate it throughout to the work of other key sociologists and social theorists.

## SOCIOLOGICAL ENLIGHTENMENT

Niklas Luhmann was born in the German city of Lüneburg on 8 December 1927, thereby belonging to the same generation as other key modern sociologists such as Pierre Bourdieu (1930–2002) and Jürgen Habermas (b. 1929). The most important biographical detail of Luhmann's early life is that he was drafted for the German Luftwaffe at age 15, and against his will. Luhmann and his family were sternly opposed to the Nazi regime, and the experience with totalitarianism had a deep normative impact on Luhmann's later theorising: although it was a virtue for Luhmann to be explicitly non-normative in his sociological work, he was always normatively in favour of modern society's differentiation into autonomous function systems since this differentiation was society's bulwark against collapsing into totalitarianism. Yet Luhmann suffered from no misconceptions; the differentiation of society did not entail any guarantees that no harms be done. He knew this from another formative experience from his youth. At the end of World War II Luhmann was captured by American forces and, what at first sight might have marked a welcome liberation from the Nazi regime, soon turned out to add to the negative experiences. Luhmann thus felt on his own body how the treatment of the prisoners of war violated international conventions (Luhmann in Horster 1997: 28). This taught him that notions such as 'good' and 'bad' should only be used cautiously to assess political regimes (Luhmann 1987a: 129).

After the war Luhmann studied law and then worked for some years in the public administration. Alongside this work he pursued scholarly interests and published some articles on administration and organisations. The academic interest was further encouraged by a scholarship that Luhmann received and which allowed him to go to Talcott Parsons at Harvard University in 1960–1. Although Luhmann was familiar with sociological theory prior to his stay at Harvard, Parsons inspired him to cultivate the sociological interest – and to explore in detail the kind of functionalist approach that Parsons advocated. The result was not late in coming. Some of Luhmann's first publications after he returned from the USA thus discussed the sociological advantages of functionalism (Luhmann 1962; 1964).

There are important differences between Luhmann's and Parsons' understandings of functionalism, however. Parsons developed a comprehensive structural-functionalist theory which argued that a social system is characterised by certain structures (a shared value system, as he called it), and that it can only be maintained if it fulfils specific functions. This focus on the maintenance of the system motivated the critique that

Parsons' sociological programme was inherently conservative; it did not adequately account for possible changes of the system. Contrary to Parsons Luhmann did not begin with structure. Rather his approach revolved around function, hence his argument that he enacted a trans-formation from (Parsonian) structural functionalism to a functionalist-structural systems theory (e.g. Luhmann 1967a). More specifically, Luhmann's main point was to attribute a very different meaning to function than Parsons did. Thus, for Luhmann, functionalism refers to an essentially comparative approach which studies the possible relations between problems and solutions. That is, rather than operating with a strict causality between a given problem and its solution, Luhmann argued that sociology could use functionalism to look for functionally equivalent alternatives. If, for example, we are used to observing climate change as a problem that requires political solutions, Luhmann's func-tionalist approach invites us to look for and compare alternative ways to solve this problem, be they of economic, scientific, legal, etc. form. In that sense the functional method seeks to provide new ways of conceiving the social world.

The fellowship at Harvard inspired Luhmann to pursue an academic career. He therefore left the administration to take up a position at the Academy for Administrative Sciences in Speyer, Germany, in 1962. Two years later he published his first major book, *Funktionen und Folgen formaler Organisation* (1964), through which Luhmann made his mark as a central organisation theorist in Germany. Luhmann's intellectual capacities were easily seen, and it did not take long before one of Germany's most influential sociologists at the time, Professor Helmut Schelsky, invited him to join him at Münster University and to be part of the Center for Social Research in Dortmund which Schelsky led from Münster. Besides being one of Germany's most prominent soci-ologists, Schelsky was also deeply involved in instituting Bielefeld University. In particular, Schelsky played an important role in estab-lishing in Bielefeld the first distinctive faculty of sociology in Germany. It was at this new faculty that Luhmann was appointed professor in 1969. He retired in 1993, but retained his affiliation with Bielefeld University till he died on 6 November 1998.

Shortly before moving to Bielefeld Luhmann held a programmatic inaugural lecture at Münster University. The title of the talk was 'Sociological Enlightenment' (1967b), indicating that Luhmann conceived of his own sociology as standing on the shoulders of the Enlightenment tradition. Yet, argued Luhmann, a contemporary conception of enlight-enment would have to move significantly beyond the classical under-standings of the term. In particular, he asserted, the complexity of society is now so great that recourse to reason, the most celebrated Enlightenment notion, can no longer serve as the ultimate solution to societal problems. As an alternative approach Luhmann suggested that sociology should operate, not as applied enlightenment, i.e. as promoting reason as the grand answer to every problem, but rather as a 'serene enlightenment' (*abgeklärte Aufklärung*) which would imply being aware of the limits to enlightenment (1967b: 98).

Not surprisingly, this refined notion of enlightenment referred to Luhmann's own systems–theoretical programme. Specifically, he associated it with a formula which became almost synonymous with his early work, namely 'reduction of complexity'. In what might be termed the cosmology underlying all of Luhmann's work, he argued that the social world comprises enormous complexity which social systems, each in their own way, reduce. This was in effect the early definition of social systems he proposed: a system is something that reduces the complexity of its environment. This is why it makes sense to talk of the economy or science as social systems. Even if they are extremely complex in themselves, they nonetheless suggest ways in which the social complexity is radically reduced. Thus the economy proposes a view on the social world in which the latter's complexity is reduced to matters of payments, interest rates, capital, etc. Likewise, the system of science suggests theories and methods with which to address (and reduce) the complexity of the world. It is important to stress that, for Luhmann, the reduction of complexity, and hence the formation of systems, is an indispensable and unavoidable occurrence. Since the complexity of the world is so overwhelming, we can only arrive at a meaningful way of living if we somehow reduce the complexity. Sociological systems theory shows not only that this is the case, but also how the reduction of complexity unfolds.

It was this idea of complexity reduction that Luhmann linked to his notion of enlightenment. Thus, in Luhmann's interpretation, enlightenment is neither about collecting more knowledge, nor is it about promoting reason. In fact, Luhmann argued, such a classical understanding of enlightenment ignores that the mere accumulation of knowledge might increase complexity rather than reduce it. As an illustration of this limit to enlightenment, as Luhmann conceived it, one might refer to contemporary suggestions for how to live a healthy life. Evermore research produces still new recommendations for what (not) to eat, how (not) to behave, etc. While the stockpiling of all this information is consistent with Enlightenment ideals, the research findings often contradict one another (one day a particular kind of food is considered healthy, the next day it is not). This means that instead of offering guidelines for behaviour, the accumulation of knowledge actually increases complexity.

Luhmann believed his functionalist systems theory to be more apt. Rather than promoting knowledge and reason for their own sake, this theoretical apparatus claimed to understand how social systems may 'increase their potential for grasping and reducing complexity' (1967b: 123). Furthermore, since social systems reduce the complexity in different ways, this systemic perspective also implied taking seriously that no single Reason (with a capital R) exists. Rather, and this is another of Luhmann's key mantras, the reduction of complexity is always characterised by *contingency*, i.e. by being 'neither necessary nor impossible', as Luhmann liked to put it (1998c: 45). It is always possible to think of different ways to understand and approach the world (and hence to reduce complexity).

The emphasis on contingency is closely linked to Luhmann's functionalist method which also played a crucial role in his programme for a sociological enlightenment. By distinguishing between what is latent and what is manifest, Luhmann argued that in addition to the actual (manifest) way that complexity may be reduced in a specific context, one can point to latent (functionally equivalent) options that might equally be utilised. For Luhmann, sociological enlightenment therefore amounts to making this latency manifest, i.e. showing that society need not submit to the 'truths' of a given time and context, but that other possible solutions exist which systems theory invites sociologists to consider, compare and reflect upon.

## THE DEBATE WITH HABERMAS

Early on Luhmann became a well-known figure within German sociology. This was not entirely his own accomplishment, but partly an effect of a famous confrontation he had with Jürgen Habermas, the key voice of critical theory in the 1960s and 1970s. Luhmann's ambiguous ties with the Frankfurt School were founded in the late 1960s (ambiguous in the sense that, while his theory was in clear opposition to the Frankfurt School's critical line of thinking, he also benefited from the encounter). During a strike in Frankfurt, Luhmann thus briefly held Theodor W. Adorno's chair in Frankfurt in 1968–69, which is interesting for at least two reasons. First of all, it is completely unthinkable, as Thomas Anz (2009) notes, that Luhmann was invited to substitute for Adorno without the latter's and Habermas' explicit consent. This bears witness to a commendable openness on the side of the Frankfurt scholars to take seriously and engage with a position which they considered almost perpendicular to their own. Second, during his rather short time in Frankfurt Luhmann offered a seminar on love and wrote a brief text on love as a preparation for the seminar. This text was published posthumously in 2008 (Luhmann 2008b), although its main essence has been known for years, as it was elaborated in the 1982 book on *Love as Passion* (1998a).[1] The interesting thing to note here is the irony – perhaps intended on Luhmann's side – that, as Anz observes, it was Luhmann, the administration and organisation theorist associated with dull conservative functionalism, who offered a seminar on love, whereas the topic Habermas was teaching his students at the time was 'organization and bureaucracy' (Anz 2009; see also Kluge 2009: 497–517; Precht 2009).

In any case, the stay in Frankfurt naturally brought Luhmann in contact with the local critical theory environment. The arguably most significant outcome of this was the debate with Habermas he engaged in, and which culminated in a book they published together in 1971, entitled *Theorie der Gesellschaft order Sozialtechonologie. Was leistet die Systemforschung?* [*Theory of Society or Social Technology: What Does Systems Research Attain?*].

The title of the book nicely captured the main point of disagreement. Luhmann strongly believed that his systems theory offered a new, alternative theory of society, i.e. a theory which was able to grasp the complexity of the social world. For Luhmann, this theoretical framework held the potentials to revolutionise sociology. Habermas, on his side, did not see any revolutionary potential in systems theory. Quite the opposite, in Habermas' eyes, Luhmann's work mainly qualified as a piece of social technology, i.e. as a technocratic endeavour which by its very nature contributed to reproducing the existing order and hence the existing forms of domination. In other words, Habermas did not believe that Luhmann represented any critique of society, and for this reason, he believed, systems theory collapsed into an ideological defence of the societal structure at hand (Habermas 1971: 266–7). This attack was not exactly offset by the fact that Luhmann was under the wings of Schelsky and pursued an interest in functionalist systems theory which, at the time, was associated with the name of Parsons. Both Schelsky and Parsons had a reputation of being conservative sociologists, meaning that Luhmann's affiliation with these scholars added to the image that he too represented a conservative position.

Luhmann rejected the critique that his systems theory embodied a conservative approach (Luhmann 1971b: 398–405). He argued that, in a rapidly changing society like the present one, it hardly makes sense anymore to distinguish sharply between conservative and progressive positions. On the one hand, the altering nature of society means that inventive work is required to prevent the flux from changing all societal domains. In other words, one has to be extremely progressive to preserve structures. On the other hand, progressive ideals often fall back on outdated conceptions which do not correspond to the present societal order. This argument was aimed provocatively at the Habermas camp which, for Luhmann, subscribed to an essentially conservative strand of thinking, in spite of its explicitly critical-progressive ambitions. For example, Luhmann claimed, the critical theory that Habermas represented incarnated a kind of 'emancipation conservatism' (Reese-Schäfer 1992: 142); it referred back to a notion of emancipation which presupposed the existence of a subject that could and should be liberated from repressing social structures. In Luhmann's eyes, this emphasis on emancipation signified the preservation of an old and antiquated vocabulary that is no longer apt if we want to adequately understand the complexity of the social world, which cannot be reduced to an opposition between systems and subjects. Luhmann believed that his guiding theoretical distinction between systems and their environment avoided such misconceptions.

This point of disagreement largely concerned the political role of sociology, but it also reflected other important differences. For example, in spite of the fact that Luhmann's lecture on sociological enlightenment on first sight associated him with the rationality agenda which Habermas also endorsed, this covered over considerable disparities. Significantly, Luhmann did not share Habermas' belief in the progressive function of reason as a countermeasure to domination.[2] As mentioned above, he adopted a critical approach to the alleged salvation through reason and argued instead for a modified notion of (serene) enlightenment. This, moreover, illuminated an important stylistic difference between Habermas and Luhmann. Whereas Habermas and the critical theorists put forward a passionate critique of modern, capitalist society and its repressive tendencies, Luhmann assumed a much colder attitude. His insistence on notions such as systems, complexity reduction and functionalism did not exactly inspire political engagement. Quite the contrary, this technical vocabulary easily lent itself to the critique that Luhmann was preoccupied with technocratic concerns, far remote from the daily sufferings and injustices that people might experience. In a sense this was correct. Luhmann did not envision any political mobilisation to arise from his theorising. His ambitions remained scientific and, more specifically, theoretical. This, Luhmann reasoned, was more important than promoting a normative political programme that was based on what he considered insufficient theoretical grounds.

Luhmann's preference for a cold theoretical approach and the advantages he saw in pursuing theoretical rather than empirical work are nicely described in the Preface to his book on *Ecological Communication* (to be discussed in Chapter 5):

> Investigations that are inspired theoretically can always be accused of a lack of 'practical reference'. They do not provide prescriptions for others to use. They observe practice and occasionally ask what is to be gained by making such a hasty use of incomplete ideas. This does not exclude the possibility that serviceable results can be attained in this way. But then the significance of the theory will always remain that a more controlled method of creating ideas can increase the probability of more serviceable results – above all, that *it can reduce the probability of creating useless excitement.*
>
> (1989a: xviii, italics added)

It is this coldness, this consequent denial to be carried away by politically informed excitement and easy moral judgements, that has endowed his work with an unmistakably cynical (Luhmann would say sober) attitude. While the majority of Luhmann's work is characterised by this cold, technical-theoretical, non-normative stance – often spiced up with irony – he acted out of character, as it were, on a few occasions. One is, as previously indicated, his ardent defence of modern society's functional differentiation, a differentiation he regarded a bulwark against the totalitarianism which he, similar to Habermas, was eager to deflect. Another example of a warmer and more engaged approach is his discussions of inclusion and exclusion from the 1990s. Based on personal experiences from the Brazilian *favelas*, Luhmann here expressed his concern that inclusion/exclusion might become the new guiding difference of society in the future. As an indication of this concern, Luhmann even pointed to possible measures on how to handle this challenge. I shall return to his inclusion/exclusion reflections as well as to his more or less concealed normativities in later chapters.

The debate between Luhmann and Habermas may have culminated in the 1970s, but it continued with varying intensity until Luhmann's death in 1998. For Habermas, Luhmann's systems theory retained its status as a theoretical position that should be taken very seriously, but which left hardly any possibilities for societal critique. One example of this critical analysis of Luhmann is his *Philosophical Discourse of Modernity*, an important book in which Habermas presented original interpretations of key social thinkers from Hegel and Nietzsche over Adorno and Horkheimer to Foucault and Luhmann (Habermas 1987). In his discussion of Luhmann, Habermas rightly observed that, according to

Luhmann's theory (especially as it developed in the 1980s), modern society is differentiated into an a-centric wealth of function systems, each following their own logics and rationalities. In such a society there is no overarching rationality, only system-specific rationalities. But, Habermas stated, 'if modern societies have no possibility whatsoever of shaping a rational identity', i.e. if no recourse can be made to common intersubjective form of rationality, 'then we are without any point of reference for a critique of modernity' (1987: 374). Put differently, for Habermas, Luhmann's systems theory retained a conservative bias.

On Luhmann's side, throughout the 1980s and 1990s, the critique against the Habermasian horizon often appears as snide remarks. But there are also occasions where he situated his work vis-à-vis Habermas' position in more elaborated terms. One example is Luhmann's 1991 article 'Am Ende der kritischen Soziologie' ['The End of Critical Sociology']. In this article, published shortly after the breakdown of Soviet communism, Luhmann put forward a fundamental critique of Habermas' critical project. This critique did not use the collapse of communism as a way to pull the carpet from under the leftwing project of Habermas. One could not draw any such direct sociological implications from political events, Luhmann warned (1991: 147). Rather, his attack on Habermas revolved around ontological and epistemological issues. Thus, stated Luhmann, critical theory had always assumed a superior, know-all attitude in that it believed it was able to describe the social reality in a way that was truer than how other sociologists or 'ordinary' people observed it (hence the old notion of false consciousness).

According to Luhmann, this way of approaching the reality amounted to what he termed first-order observation, i.e. a kind of (ontological) observation of what the world *is*. Luhmann had only little sympathy with the idea that it is possible to possess 'the true' view on society which may then be applied as a benchmark for doing societal critique. Any ontological observation can be challenged, he thought.[3] For this reason he argued for shifting from first-order observation to second-order observation, which refers to observing *how* other observers (for instance, critical sociologists) observe. According to Luhmann, this produced a shift from ontology to epistemology (to be explored in more detail in Chapter 3). More importantly for the present discussion, this shift also implied a fundamental transformation of the notion of critique: Rather than starting with the idea that the social world *is* constituted in this or that way, and which may then be critiqued as illegitimate, unfair, repressive, etc., he argued for a critical observation of *how* observers observe the constitution of society. While Habermas would characterise this move as yet another indication of Luhmann's lacking ability to offer a critique of society, Luhmann would celebrate it as a much more refined and adequate way of approaching the social reality. Instead of criticising specific social structures as they 'really' are, this second-order perspective thus points to the need for assessing how societal problems and concerns are constructed.

Luhmann's shift to second-order observations also formed the backdrop to a polemic lecture he held at a conference devoted to assessing the relevance of the Frankfurt School and published under the title 'I See Something You Don't See' (Luhmann 2002g). This text applied the second-order analysis to the observations of the Frankfurt scholars. The result was devastating. Luhmann thus argued that the concepts which Habermas and his colleagues employed to observe modern society were 'obviously exhausted', as they were derived (uncritically) from the Enlightenment and the French Revolution (Luhmann 2002g: 192). Put differently, the Frankfurt School made use of a vocabulary that referred back to the time where society was undergoing a profound *transition* into its modern formation. Describing contemporary society on basis of such an old (and, in Luhmann's view, obsolete) terminology could only produce inadequate results. A conceptual apparatus that could describe modern society in more apt and contemporary terms would therefore have to be found elsewhere, not least, Luhmann thought, in sociological systems theory.

These and other comments on Habermas' work bear witness to an increasing self-confidence on Luhmann's side. It thus seems that from the late 1980s onward, Luhmann freed himself from the mainly defensive position he occupied in the 1970s. Indeed, whereas Habermas was generally perceived to have had the upper hand in the debate throughout the 1970s, things gradually changed. A major turning point was the theoretical programme Luhmann set out in his 1984 book *Soziale Systeme* (translated into English as *Social Systems* in 1995). Luhmann conceived of this book as marking a paradigm shift within sociology. The book certainly instigated a fresh perspective which was received positively by many German scholars and seen as a new start for theoretical deliberation. As a result Hans-Georg Moeller has noted, '[i]n a somewhat dialectic turn of the tide, Habermasian social theory had become the established creed of aging leftist intellectuals, while Luhmann's work was now perceived as having an innovative and avant-gardist approach' (2006: 188). If one accepts the distinction between progressives and conservatives, Luhmann, the allegedly conservative theorist of the 1970s, was now seen to be the progressive one.

The confrontation with Habermas produced instant recognition of Luhmann's work in the sense that if Habermas spent time engaging in a critical discussion of Luhmann's systems theory, this obviously indicated that this theory was in fact worth debating. But even if both camps generally maintained a sober attitude and respected one another's arguments, this did not imply any agreement on substance. The opposition between the two positions was and remained firm. Still, Luhmann could and did use the confrontation to position himself in the German academic landscape in the 1970s. Later on he found greater interest in situating his sociological work vis-à-vis other positions, in particular that of the French philosopher Jacques Derrida. I shall return to this below and in Chapter 3.

## LUHMANN'S OEUVRE: PHASES AND RECEPTION

I mentioned Luhmann's impressive production at the beginning of the chapter and his productivity is indeed legendary. So is one of the main technical means he deployed to maintain this productivity, namely his file-card system, the so-called *Zettelkästen*. Luhmann began working on this file-card system in the early 1950s and kept expanding it throughout his career. Briefly put, the idea of this system was to write down ideas on clearly numerically identifiable paper files. These ideas often came from reading, say, from Luhmann's reading of Parsons. Each file could refer to other files, making up a highly non-linear cross-referencing system. When Luhmann was about to prepare an article or book chapter on some topic, he would line up all the file-cards referring to the topic and then begin ordering and re-ordering the card-files. By combining card-files in novel ways, new cross-references would emerge leading to new ways to approach the topic at hand. Luhmann has described how the re-combination of card-files produced new levels of creativity where the article or chapter more or less grew out of the card-files (1987a: 142–5; 1992a). It was this working method that enabled him to retain his enormous productivity which, significantly, has even continued with the publication of several books after he passed away. This posthumous work has been provided for by some of Luhmann's former colleagues who have edited the manuscripts Luhmann left.

It is possible to distinguish between separate phases in Luhmann's enormous sociological production. Often his work is divided into two main parts (e.g. Kneer and Nassehi 1993: 34). The first phase, which is associated with the notion of functionalism, runs from his earliest writings to the 1984 breakthrough he received with *Soziale Systeme*. This book marks the beginning of the second phase which is associated with the notion of autopoiesis and by giving priority to communication as the fundamental social fact.

Luhmann has contributed to cementing this division into two major parts of his work. For example, he has claimed that *Soziale Systeme* was a point zero in his theoretical work in the sense that it laid down the first stone in his new conception of how a theory of society must be constructed (Luhmann in Horster 1997: 42; Luhmann 1987a: 142). Additional building blocks came later on, not least in the form of a series of books devoted to specific function systems (economy, law, science, art, politics, religion, etc.), but the fundamental framework was now set.

The division of Luhmann's work into a functionalist and an autopoietic phase is warranted, but it also hides over some complex transformations within the post-1984 publications. I will therefore argue that, in order to fully understand Luhmann's work, it makes sense to speak of a third phase. When scrutinising Luhmann's work published after *Soziale Systeme* it is thus apparent that, although he remained within the general autopoietic framework, his theory took a new course from the late 1980s onward. At this time he became increasingly interested in the notion of observation and developed a whole new vocabulary around this concept. As a part of this new interest, which gave priority to epistemological issues, Luhmann rephrased many older theoretical notions in observation terms. In the present book I am mainly interested in Luhmann's work from the 1980s and 1990s, as it is this work which most strongly defines Luhmann as a key sociologist.

In spite of the various phases that may be identified in Luhmann's thought, there are also important continuities. One is an interest in historical studies in the sociology of knowledge which he published as a series entitled *Gesellschaftsstruktur und Semantik* [*Societal Structure and Semantics*]. The aim of these studies was to investigate the vocabulary, the semantics, with which society describes itself. More specifically, in this part of his work, Luhmann was interested in how a society's structure, defined as its primary mode of differentiation, makes certain semantics plausible. In particular, Luhmann attempted to analyse the semantic effects of the transition from traditional (stratified/hierarchically differentiated) to modern (functionally differentiated) society. As he once described the contours of this sociology of knowledge:

> This project starts from the assumption that the basic semantic terms used to describe either society or time underwent a radical change during the second half of the eighteenth century; even words which remained the same took on new meanings. Historians, however, have not explained the reasons for this transformation, but have merely confirmed that it did indeed occur.
>
> (1998a: 2)

Luhmann wanted to understand and describe what the historians failed to account for, and he did so in detailed – and for a change – *empirical* studies. The first volume in this project was published in 1980; the fourth and final one came out in 1995. Although not formally part of this series, the sociology of knowledge project also includes Luhmann's book on *Love as Passion* (1998a). This book describes the development of love semantics and demonstrates how the transition to modern, functionally differentiated society gave way to new forms of intimate communication.

Another book series that spanned over most of Luhmann's career was called *Sociological Enlightenment*, consisting of altogether six volumes that were mainly composed of articles that had already appeared elsewhere. Although this series carried the name of Luhmann's inaugural lecture from 1967, the various volumes focused on specific topics (such as functional differentiation and constructivism) that were only indirectly related to the programmatic lecture, and which were treated in ways that reflected the development of his sociological theory. Finally, and on a more collaborative basis, beginning in the early 1980s Luhmann published a series of books on systems-theoretical contributions to pedagogy with Karl Eberhard Schorr.

In addition to these series Luhmann produced numerous books and articles on all sorts of topics (on power, trust, organisations, risk, etc.). This work may not be categorised within specific series, but it all formed part of Luhmann's overall programme: to develop a grand theory of society. This ambition to develop a grand theory of society was pursued in particular in a stream of books published in the second and third phases of his career. This was set off with the book on *Social Systems*, which was followed by a sequence of books devoted to each of the subsystems of society. The titles of these books demonstrated their connection to the common project: *Die Wirtschaft der Gesellschaft* (1988b), *Die Wissenschaft der Gesellschaft* (1990a), *Das Recht der Gesellschaft* (1993a), *Die Kunst der Gesellschaft* (1995a) as well as the posthumous *Die Politik der Gesellschaft* (2000b), *Die Religion der Gesellschaft* (2000c) and *Das Erziehungssystem der Gesellschaft* (2002b) – in English: *Society's Economy*, *Society's Science*, *Society's Law* (the official English translation is *Law as a Social System*, 2004), *Society's Art* (official English translation is *Art as a Social System*, 2000a), *Society's Politics*, *Society's Religion*, *Society's Educational System*. The culmination was the two-volume masterpiece, *Die Gesellschaft der Gesellschaft* (1997a, *Society's Society*).

Only a fraction of Luhmann's oeuvre has been translated into English. Although the books and articles that have been translated cover all phases of his work and as such provide a sober picture of his research interests, it seems fair to say that Luhmann's work has never received the breakthrough in the English-speaking world that many believe it deserves. Let me therefore end this introductory chapter with a few words on the reception of Luhmann's sociological theory.

There is no doubt that Luhmann's uncompromising theoretical ambitions, including his aim to propose a grand theory of society (grand theorising being a rather German specialty), is mainly attractive to other similarly theoretically inclined minds. Accordingly, much of the existing reception of Luhmann has continued along the theoretical path he set out. Except from his semantic studies there is hardly any systematic empirical analysis in Luhmann, at least not in a classical manner (no interviews, no systematic ethnographic work, no questionnaires, etc.). This merely reflects Luhmann's own preferences, however, and does not preclude empirical applications of systems theory. Thus, in recent years a number of empirical studies have emerged that draw on Luhmann's work (e.g. Andersen 2008; 2009; Højlund 2009).

As mentioned above, Luhmann's enormous production includes analyses of politics, law, love, pedagogy, art, science, religion, organisations, etc. This has paved the way for a reception of systems theory, not only within sociology proper, but also outside of the sociological discipline. In particular, Luhmann's work has been debated within legal theory, political science, organisation studies, aesthetic theory and pedagogical research.[4] When viewed from a geographical angle, it appears that much of this discussion has taken place in German-speaking countries, although a strong interest in Luhmann can also be observed in the Scandinavian countries, in the Netherlands, and in Italy as well as in Chile. Interestingly, however, so far only relatively little discussion has emerged in the English-speaking countries, and less in the USA than in the UK. Moreover, in the USA, Luhmann hardly forms part of the sociological canon, but mainly attracts attention in Law, German or Literature departments.

One might speculate that this reception pattern has to do with some strategic choices that Luhmann made and which concern the conversation partners he picked. While Luhmann used Habermas as a prominent antagonist in the 1970s, he increasingly positioned himself in relation to Derrida and the interest in deconstruction that the latter inspired. For many continental European social theorists, it was Derrida rather than Habermas who set the theoretical agenda in the 1980s and 1990s. So from a strategic point of view it made great sense for Luhmann to relate his work to that of Derrida and to capitalise on the commonalities between systems theory and deconstruction. Yet whereas Derrida was taken seriously in many European sociology departments, the situation was rather different in the United States, where deconstruction was mainly discussed in literature departments. So in addition to pursuing a kind of grand theory which, since Parsons, was never in vogue in the American sociological landscape, it might be argued that Luhmann's positioning vis-à-vis Derrida unwittingly helped create a barrier to a more positive and comprehensive reception of his work among American sociologists. Be that as it may. As I hope to demonstrate in this book, irrespective of the reception, Luhmann offers an intriguing, if complex, view of society which should be taken seriously, both because of the analyses it provides, and because of the questions it raises for existing sociological thinking.

# 2

# Social systems

'The following considerations assume that there are systems', reads the famous opening sentence in Chapter 1 of Luhmann's *Social Systems* (1995g: 12). This sentence, which could just as well have read, 'Let there be systems!', points to the simple operation that triggers his entire sociological theory: The world is cut in two, namely into a system and its environment. While this seems to be an innocent starting point, the implications of this separation are far from simple, as I will show in this chapter. In his examination of what the distinction between system and environment entails, Luhmann thus arrives at a new and surprising view of society. Often, he states (1997a: 24–5), sociologists implicitly or explicitly subscribe to one or more of the following suppositions:

1.  that a society consists of concrete human beings and relations between human beings;
2.  that society is consequently constituted or at least integrated by consensus between human beings, correspondence of their opinions, and complementarity of their goal definitions;
3.  that societies are regional and territorially limited units, so that Brazil is a different society from Thailand, the US different from Russia, and then, supposedly, also Uruguay a different society from Paraguay;
4.  and that therefore societies can be observed from the outside just as groups of people or territories.

(Quoted from the English translation
in Moeller 2006: 229–30)

Yet these assumptions lead to a deceptive view of society, Luhmann claims (1997a: 32; Luhmann in Moeller 2006: 236). For example, the emphasis on the human subject includes too much in the conception of society (in what sense is my left foot part of society?), just as the territorial definition includes too little (does it make sense to distinguish between local societies in a globalised world?). By changing the focus from humans to social systems an entirely new (and more adequate) notion of society and the social comes into view.[1] But what is a social system, how does it operate, and what conception of society emerges on this basis?

## WHAT IS A SYSTEM?

To answer these questions it is helpful to note that Luhmann situates his sociological analysis of social systems within a broader framework usually designated with the term general systems theory. As this notion indicates, general systems theory seeks to account for the general features of systems (how they function and operate), independently of their specific form. Luhmann employs a number of findings from general systems theory in his own work, the most important of which will be discussed below. At the same time Luhmann's main interest is not in how systems *in general* function, but rather in how *social* systems operate. He therefore differentiates between a number of generic types of systems which, in addition to the features that are common to all systems, have qualities which are species specific, so to speak. Luhmann suggests the following typology which points to an increasing level of specification (see Figure 2.1).

As a sociologist Luhmann is not interested in how living systems (e.g. cells or immune systems) operate. Nor is he concerned with the organisation of psychic systems for their own sake, but merely in how they constitute an important environment for social systems (more on the relation between social and psychic systems follows below). Still, the

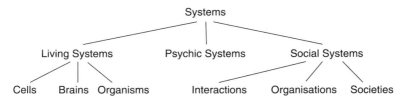

*Figure 2.1* A Typology of Systems (the figure is adapted from Luhmann, 1990a: 2; 1995g: 2).

question remains: what is, more specifically, a system? And how is the particular type of *social* systems characterised?

First of all, Luhmann asserts, we cannot speak of a system without recognising that it must first be separated from its environment. No system is possible without this initial distinction. It is on the basis of this separation that the system acquires its unity and can begin to operate on its own. It is not possible, for instance, to speak of a corporation if one cannot distinguish it from its environment. If anything blends into everything else and no clear boundaries can be established, then no system exists. To put it in an ontological vocabulary, one could say that *the system 'is' nothing but the difference to its environment* (Luhmann 2002a: 66).

It follows from this that the system assumes a special relationship to its environment. It is different from, but also could not exist without the environment.[2] But, and this relates to its internal organisation, the distinction between system and environment also implies that, even if the system requires an environment from which it can separate itself, everything that goes on in the system is the system's own matter and only takes place within the system's boundaries (see Figure 2.2).

To make a crude illustration, a group of punks might be seen as constituting a system that separates itself from its (conformist) environment. The systemic character of these punks consists in their independent lifestyle, tastes, attitudes, etc., which are produced and reproduced within the group. If it were not possible for the punks to maintain their difference to the rest of society, they would fall apart as a system. This applies to all systems; they only exist to the extent that they are able to differentiate themselves from their environment.

The distinction between system and environment has other important implications. Thus, just as the system is dependent on its environment, so the environment is always system specific. This follows from the assertion that each system emerges on the basis of its own

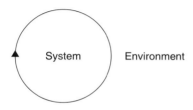

*Figure 2.2* System and Environment.

environment. Consequently, the environment 'is different for every system, because every system excludes only itself from its environment' (1995g: 17). Hence, the environment for the system of punks differs from that of a system of wine enthusiasts.

Furthermore, the distinction between system and environment implies that the environment is no system. This is no trivial statement, but refers to the central claim that 'the environment has no self-reflection or capacity to act'; these are capacities that are reserved exclusively for systems (1995g: 17). This does not preclude systems from attributing all sorts of actions to their environment. For example, punks might argue that opposition is needed because non-punks behave conformist. Yet, this remains an attribution that the *system* makes, not the environment.

Finally, it is crucial not to conflate the distinction between system and environment with that between a system and the systems in its environment. That is, system/environment is not to be confused with system/ system relations. Every system is differentiated from its environment, but this environment may contain other systems. Indeed, states Luhmann, the social world is made up of a vast plurality of systems and many systems are related to one another in different ways. However, since these systems have separate boundaries, they are not in a position to determine how other systems operate or how they relate to their specific environment. The interrelations between systems will be examined later on. Before so doing, it is important to understand the internal organisation of systems which Luhmann analyses through notions such as operational closure, self-organisation, autopoiesis and self-reference.

## OPERATIONAL CLOSURE AND SELF-ORGANISATION

Very generally defined a system is an entity whose elements are related to one another in a certain manner (Kneer and Nassehi 1993: 17–18). But what do these elements consist of and how to describe their relatedness? Following the systems typology above (Figure 2.1), Luhmann argues that living systems are characterised by operations that focus on life; the operations of psychic systems are constituted by consciousness; whereas social systems are characterised by having communications as their distinctive type of operations (see Figure 2.3).

Due to the boundaries between the systems, these operations cannot travel from one system to another. Social systems cannot suddenly incorporate operations from the immune system; although, of course, social systems can use their own operations, communications, to discuss how the organism works. The situation is not fundamentally different for systems that use the same general kind of operation. Thus, even if all

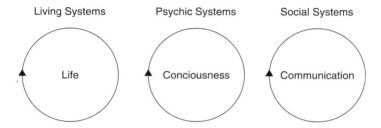

*Figure 2.3* System Operations.

social systems have communication as their essential type of operation, no social system can interfere in the operations of other social systems, which is another way of saying that no system can cross its own boundaries. The inability to incorporate operations from the outside is a consequence of the systems' so-called *operational closure*. Every system is closed around its specific operations. For example, Luhmann argues that science constitutes an operationally independent social system which has particular ways of relating its elements to one another. Specifically, he states, the system of science operates with communications about what is true and what is false, and it employs theories and methods to decide when a statement should be considered either true or false. Likewise, the legal system is specialised in communicating about whether acts should be considered legal or illegal. The operational closure of these systems means that the system of science cannot accept the legal system's operations as its own, and vice versa. A legal judgment is not a scientific judgment, and legal procedures are not scientific procedures.

It is important to note that closure only refers to the operational level and only to the fact that no system can operate beyond its boundaries. Therefore, 'closure does not mean empirical isolation', as Luhmann is careful to stress over and over again (1992b: 1431). There are two reasons for this. First, every system is embedded in the world and no system could exist without some environmental support. For example, there could be no social systems, no communication, if there were no living organisms and no psychic systems. Luhmann describes these environmental or ecological requirements, which cannot be fulfilled by the system itself, as a 'materiality continuum', i.e. as the external material conditions of possibility for social systems (1997a: 100). Second, operational closure does not entail empirical isolation because the operational closure is followed by cognitive openness. Indeed, Luhmann claims in another of his many paradoxical formulations, social systems are open toward their environment *because* (not in spite) of their operational closure (see, e.g. Luhmann 2002a: 93). It is this closure that enables systems to perceive their environment, although this perception will always be processed according to the system's own internal premises. For instance, it is the operational closure of the system of science that enables legal scholars to observe and communicate scientifically about legal decisions. Similarly, it is the operational closure of the group of punks that provides them with the ability to look beyond their own boundary and start reflect on things that happen in their environment. So, to repeat the point, social systems are cognitively open systems, because they are operationally closed.

Operational closure produces and reproduces the system's boundary: the system emerges when a difference to its environment is established, and this is a difference which is operationally produced and needs operational reproduction if the system's existence is to be ensured. It was mentioned above that a system's elements are related to one another in a specific manner. This means that the operational reproduction does not occur coincidentally; rather, it follows the system's structural set up which Luhmann describes with the notion of *self-organisation*. To be a self-organising system implies that, similar to the operations, the structure is internally produced and cannot be imported from the outside. Luhmann is well aware that a certain circularity is at stake between operations and structure. The operations demand a structure, but this structure is a result of the operations. He illustrates this by pointing to the relation between language (structure) and speech (operation). Language is the precondition for speech. Without language there would be no speech, but only, if at all, sounds and utterances. At the same time, language is produced by the operations of speech. If nobody were speaking the language, it would collapse. So language (structure) and speech (operations) co-constitute one another circularly. This co-constitution is not a fixed thing; rather it is subject to a complex developmental logic. Luhmann therefore asserts that in practice systems develop on the basis of operations that only demand minimal structural capacity, which then create more complex structures that allow for still more differentiated operations, and so on (Luhmann 2002a: 108–9).

It is important to note that Luhmann's concept of structure does not refer to, for example, the basic economic structure of society, such as Marxism would have it. Structure, for Luhmann, refers to *expectations* which produce a stabilisation of how systems select their operations. 'Expectations come into being by constraining ranges of possibilities. Finally, they are this constraint itself' (1995g: 292). This sounds very formal and abstract, but may be illustrated in a straightforward manner. A social system of wine enthusiasts could potentially discuss any topic, be it new traffic regulation, classical music, the beauty of Vienna, etc. Yet the structure of the system constrains the relevant discussion topics to be concerned with wine, perhaps only specific wines or particular aspects of wine production. Expectations therefore function as a kind of complexity reduction; they limit what can be selected by the system.

Of course, expectations can be disappointed. For example, a new member of the system of wine enthusiasts may repeatedly digress from the wine topic and complain about the government's energy policies. The effects of such disappointments of expectations depend on the specific structure and how the system relates to it. Luhmann distinguishes between two basic forms of expectations, namely cognitive and normative expectations. *Cognitive expectations* are characterised by adaptation to the disappointment. If within the system of science it turns out that an expectation is disappointed, say, a hypothesis is not sustained when confronted with empirical data, then the system learns from this and changes its expectations (produces modified hypotheses). *Normative expectations*, by contrast, are upheld even if disappointed. For example, criminal law embodies the expectation that murder is wrong and must be punished. This expectation is retained despite the fact that some people actually disappoint the expectation and commit murders and/or escape from prison.

Not all kinds of systems are structured by expectations. According to Luhmann, this is a feature which is specific to psychic and social systems. So both consciousness and communication rely on expectations for the selection of operations. Luhmann further asserts that social systems are characterised by developing *reflexive* expectations. They not merely build expectations about occurrences, but also – and arguably much more intensively – about the expectations themselves. People guide their behaviour according to the expectations they form about expectations. In the words of Luhmann, '[e]go must be able to anticipate what alter anticipates of him to make his own anticipations and behavior agree with alter's anticipation' (1995g: 303).[3] This reflexivity ensures a stabilisation of the system's structure, which goes beyond this or that present event. Yet it also increases the complexity of how to deal with events. As Luhmann explains with reference to Erving Goffman's famous analysis of *Stigma* (1963),

> No one expects expectations about big ears or noses, the sun or the moon. […] Only the expectation that a person does not show repugnance at the length of someone else's nose can be expected. The nose itself is easy enough to anticipate; only one's attitude and behavior toward it need regulation consolidated by expecting expectations. Consequently, this advanced, highly risky type of

anticipation leads to the differentiation of a subdomain of events that can be expected – to the differentiation of social systems.

(Luhmann 1995g: 306)

To summarise, social systems are operationally closed and self-organising systems which use self-created expectation structures to guide how they select among the possible communications. As should be clear, the notion of operations is central to all of these dimensions. Systems consist of operations, and only of their *own* operations; and these operations stand in a circular relation to the structures which are at once produced by the operations and what guides these. In other words, every system is defined by and reproduced through its operations. To account for this reproduction Luhmann employs the notion of autopoiesis.

## AUTOPOIESIS, SELF-REFERENCE AND STRUCTURAL COUPLINGS

If complexity reduction was the catchphrase associated with Luhmann in the 1970s, autopoiesis was his slogan of the 1980s. The notion of autopoiesis was not invented by Luhmann himself, but adapted to his sociological theory from biological research as developed by the Chilean biologists Humberto Maturana and Francisco Varela. Taking their starting point in work Maturana conducted in the 1960s, he and Varela proposed a conception of living systems as spontaneously organised so-called autopoietic systems. The notion of autopoiesis is composed of the Greek words *auto*, self, and *poiésis*, production, and refers to the self-production of systems. More specifically, the theory of autopoiesis contends that an autopoietic system is one which produces and reproduces its components through a closed network of its components. This might look like Münchausen pulling himself up from a swamp by the hair; yet for Maturana and Varela, it is not a scam but rather a highly sophisticated way of conceiving the actual organisation of living systems. In the words of Maturana, autopoietic systems are

> networks of productions of components that (1) recursively, through their interactions, generate and realize the network that produces them; and (2) constitute, in the space in which they exist, the boundaries of this network of components that participate in the realization of the network.

(1981: 21; see also 2002: 12)

Luhmann is inspired by this notion of autopoiesis but does not accept all qualities that Maturana and Varela attribute to it. As with all of his other inspirational sources, Luhmann makes a very selective incorporation of the concept of autopoiesis which partially transforms the ideas originally associated with it. Most importantly, in Luhmann's adaptation, autopoiesis does not simply refer to the biological self-production of living systems (e.g. cells). It applies just as well to the self-production of communication (in social systems) and consciousness (in psychic systems). So when he argues that social systems are autopoietic systems, this means that these systems produce and reproduce their own basic operations, i.e. communications. This employment of autopoiesis to the social realm differs markedly from Maturana and Varela's initial intension with the notion. For them, autopoiesis was a pertinent description of living phenomena, not of communicative ones (see also Luhmann 2002a: 113).

It was mentioned in the discussion of operational closure that systems cannot incorporate operations from the outside, that is, operations which are not their own. This assertion gains further support with the notion of autopoiesis which entails that, just as a diesel-powered car cannot operate on gasoline, social systems do not recognise any operations but communication as their fuel. (To be sure, the motor analogy is only partially helpful, as social systems produce their own operations; engines do not). To repeat, social systems cannot suddenly introduce the operations of cells or the immune system; the latter remain biological operations. This follows from Luhmann's strict separation between the autopoiesis of life, consciousness and communication (e.g. Luhmann 1997c: 70). The autopoietic reproduction of life excludes any consciousness and communication; just as the autopoietic reproduction of consciousness excludes any life and communication, and autopoietic reproduction of communication excludes any life and consciousness. The autopoietic production and reproduction of communication is an exclusively social–systemic achievement and anything that is not communication belongs to the environment of social systems.

The same basic principle applies to how social systems relate to other social systems. Even if all social systems are based on an autopoietic reproduction of communication, which might lead to the impression that the operations of one social system can be incorporated by other social systems (they share the same kind of operation, after all), autopoiesis means that every social system will create its own *specific* communicative operations. Although they are both based on communication, the social systems of punks and wine enthusiasts produce their own operations and cannot suddenly operate with each other's operations. For example, meticulous deliberations on Bordeaux wines from the late 1960s are not accepted as relevant operations by the punks whose autopoietic reproduction may instead revolve around operations related to the legacy of Sex Pistols. Likewise, the autopoiesis of the scientific system means that it does not recognise, for instance, artful communication as relevant. Whether something is beautiful or not, does not matter when making scientific assessments about true or false.

The same applies to psychic systems. They consist of nothing but the operations of consciousness which are autopoietically produced and reproduced by the psychic systems. Everything that is not consciousness belongs to the environment of psychic systems. And even if all psychic systems operate through consciousness, they all establish their own specific autopoietical reproduction of consciousness. My thoughts remain my thoughts and cannot be suddenly be fused with the thoughts of another person, although we may communicate about our thoughts, but this is then a different matter, namely an occurrence in social systems.

Four additional points should be emphasised. First, as already intimated, the operative self-reproduction that autopoiesis enacts entails that a system can have only one type of operation. For example, social systems are characterised by communication only. Second, Luhmann is careful to stress that, for him, autopoiesis is not a matter of intensity or graduation. A system is neither 'fairly' nor 'extremely' autopoietic. Either it is autopoietic, or it is not, for either its operations are produced by the system itself or they are not (Luhmann 2002a: 116–7).[4] And if a social system is not autopoietic, then it is no social system at all, according to Luhmann's definition. Third, in line with the discussion of any system's ecological preconditions (its materiality continuum), autopoiesis does not imply that systems are entirely disembedded from their environment. Autopoiesis only refers to the operational level, namely to the constant production and reproduction of the system's operations. Yet this autopoiesis should not be conflated with systemic autarchy. Systems do depend on their environment, but they only relate to it in an autopoietic manner (Kneer and Nassehi 1993: 51). For example, the environment of social systems provides nutrition and warmth, but these are not themselves part of the autopoietic reproduction of communication systems. Fourth, the notion of autopoiesis is related to one of Luhmann's crucial ideas, namely that operations are *events* that vanish the very same moment they are actualised. An operation has no permanence, in other words, and this is why the continuous self-reproduction is so central to any autopoietic system. For social systems this means that they only exist in the moment that they communicate and that their continued existence depends on their ability to produce new communications. This temporal aspect is important to recognise so as to avoid the misconception that Luhmann proposes a static, conservative notion of social systems. He suggests the exact opposite: that social systems are forced into constant renewal.

Luhmann adds a further notion to the conceptual complex of operational closure, self-organisation and autopoiesis, namely that of *self-reference*. According to Luhmann, disregarding some very immature types, every system must be seen as a self-referential system; recognising this is one of the key theoretical achievements in modern systems theory, he believes. In fact, he states, '[o]ur thesis, namely, that there are systems, can now be narrowed down to: there are self-referential systems' (1995g: 13). The notion of self-reference is intimately related to the concepts of autopoiesis and operational closure. However, as is the case of the other concepts, self-reference is preconditioned by the initial separation between system and environment. It is only on the basis on this distinction that it makes sense to speak of self-reference; a system's operational modus can only be self-referential if the system is distinguished from its environment.

While the notion of self-reference is very abstract (and is intended by Luhmann to be so), self-reference is a common phenomenon in ordinary everyday life. When someone says 'I think …' or 'in my view …', then self-reference is at stake. The 'I' or 'me' refers back to some self. Within philosophy self-reference constitutes an old focal point, as discussions on reflexive subjects are essentially discussions about self-reference: the subject's ability to reflect upon him or herself entails self-reference. Since Luhmann does not want to found his sociology on a notion of the human subject, he applies the notion of self-reference in a broader non-subjectivist sense. Generally speaking, the 'concept of self-reference designates the unity that an element, a process, or a system is for itself. "For itself" means independent of the cut of observation by others' (Luhmann 1995g: 33). Within the subject-theoretical tradition this would mean that the 'I' constitutes a self-referential designation of the subject's unity, and this designation is a systemic (subject-internal) achievement that is not itself affected by how other persons conceive of 'me'. Similarly, *other-reference* (or hetero-reference) is at stake when the system refers to its environment rather than to itself. The subject tradition's equivalent to this would be 'you' or 'they'.

As said, the notion of self-reference is closely tied to other key ideas in Luhmann's systems theory. He thus asserts that

> One can call a system self-referential if it itself constitutes the elements that compose it as functional unities and runs reference to this self-constitution through all the relations among these elements, continuously reproducing its self-constitution in this way. In this sense, self-referential systems necessarily operate by self-contact; they possess no other form of environmental contact than this self-contact. The theory of recurrence is contained herein as the thesis

of the elements' indirect self-reference: the elements enable a relation through other elements back to themselves, such as an intensification of neuronal activity or a determination of actions via expecting those actions. On the level of this self-referential organization, self-referential systems are *closed* systems, for they allow no other forms of processing in their self-determination.

(Luhmann 1995g: 33–4, italics in original)

Again, this is formulated very theoretically, but refers to ideas that have been presented above: On a basic level, self-reference refers to the operational self-constitution of the autopoietic system, which only recognises its own elements as valid for the self-reproduction and hence is operationally closed around these elements. Just as a subject does not emerge as a self before he or she is able to say 'I' (or uses an equivalent marker), a system does not become a system before it can stabilise its distinction to its environment through an operational reference to itself. That is, a system is not a system if it only differentiates itself from its environment once and then disappears. It needs to refer back to its own operations in order to maintain its boundary.

So far the primary focus has been on the internal organisation of systems. The reason for spending so much energy on precisely these internal qualities is that this is where Luhmann puts his emphasis. Indeed, it is warranted to say that Luhmann's main interest in the system/environment distinction lies on the system side. Obviously, there would be no system without a corresponding environment, but systems theory largely confines itself to accounting for the systemic features.[5] I say 'largely' because Luhmann does offer some concepts that aim to understand how more specifically systems are related to their environment. The notion of a materiality continuum has already been mentioned as a relevant way of thematising how systems rely on certain ecological prerequisites. Yet Luhmann generally prefers to account for systems' relations to their environment by bringing in another notion from Maturana, namely that of *structural couplings* (e.g. Maturana 2002: 15–25).

One of the interesting features of this notion is that it allows Luhmann to evade a classical input–output model (Luhmann 1992b: 1432). System and environment do not stand in an input–output relationship where the environment produces some sort of input to the system which the system then processes so as to generate an output. In accordance with the autopoietic framework and the thesis about operational closure an input of external operations is simply not possible. While there can be no *causal* relation between system and environment, the former might depend on specific environmental traits which so to speak work as structural preconditions (rather than as operational input). This is what the notion of structural coupling captures. It refers to 'the specific form in which the system *presupposes* states or changes in its environment *and relies on them*' (Luhmann 1992b: 1432, italics added). According to the idea of structural couplings, as Luhmann conceives it, the autopoietic character of the system is retained, although this internal organisation may be exposed to external irritations and perturbations. *Irritation* should be understood here not as annoyance, but rather as an itching that calls for action. Crucially, and this follows once again from the basic autopoiesis assumption, irritations can only be precisely that – irritations. They do not determine action. In fact, Luhmann stresses, irritations are always self-irritations: even if they are provoked externally, they only appear in the system in a systemically mediated way, as a systemic construction (Luhmann 1997a: 118). Put differently, the system interprets the irritation in its own language. For example, the social system of wine enthusiasts might be irritated by new regulations that make imported wine more expensive. Even if this is triggered by external events, the irritation is observed through the lenses of the social system, just as the consequences are purely internally produced effects. Thus, it is the wine enthusiasts' own choice whether they want to try to ignore the new regulation and continue as if nothing had happened, or whether, for instance, they want to combat the regulations through lobbying efforts.

It is not only system/environment relations that are described with the notion of structural couplings. Luhmann also employs it to account for intersystem relations. In the social realm, for example, the legal and political systems are structurally coupled. Each operates according to their own internal autopoietic logics (see Chapter 4), but they are structurally coupled because none of them could exist without the other. The political system needs the legal system to enforce political decisions, just as the legal system needs the political system to formulate laws which it can then use as a backdrop when making legal decisions.

## SOCIAL SYSTEMS ARE SYSTEMS OF COMMUNICATION

I realise that so far the discussion has been rather abstract and that it has only partially addressed the social domain. I will therefore now turn to some of the features that are specific to social systems.[6] The main point to observe here is that the particular kind of operations that constitutes social systems is communication. To recapitulate, according to Luhmann, social systems are nothing but communication. In fact, he states, *society is nothing but communication*; society is the sum of social systems, the aggregation of communication, neither more nor less (e.g. Luhmann 1997a: 90).

It follows from the notion of social systems as communication that everything that is not communication is excluded from the operational realm of social systems. Another implication is that social systems are not restrained by physical boundaries (such as Maturana's notion of autopoiesis suggests). Communication is not limited to physical co-presence, for instance, but may tie together people in various parts of the world. For this reason, the above Figures 2.2 and 2.3 are misleading in the sense that they suggest that social systems carve out a space for themselves, i.e. that they enact a spatial separation from their environment. This is not the case, Luhmann contends. Indeed, he states, social systems 'are not at all spatially limited, but have a completely different, namely purely internal form of boundary' (Luhmann 1997a: 76). This boundary is determined by the communicative autopoiesis. While the idea of a-spatial communication might fit nicely to an everyday experience where people email their friends, family and colleagues around the world, the radical separation of communication and spatiality might also form an Achilles' heel in Luhmann's theory. I will come back to this issue later on. In the present context, however, I will leave this topic aside and focus instead on the positive qualities of Luhmann's notion of social systems of communication.

Luhmann's emphasis on communication as the basic element of the social reflects one of the ways in which his work goes significantly beyond that of Parsons, who otherwise was his main sociological inspiration. Following in the footsteps of Max Weber, Parsons conceived of his sociology as a theory of action. As he put it in the opening of his book on *The Social System*, Parsons' 'fundamental starting point is the concept of social systems of action' (Parsons 1951: 3). When reading Luhmann's early work, one has the feeling that he more or less subscribed to this idea of action systems. He thus argued that social systems are basically systems of actions and experiences (e.g. 1971a). This distinction refers to attribution, namely to whether a selection is attributed to the system itself (in which case Luhmann speaks of *action*) or whether the system attributes it to the environment (which amounts to *experience*). Bluntly put, to beat someone is to act, whereas to be beaten is an experience.

Although, as I shall come back to in later chapters, Luhmann occasionally retained this distinction between action and experience, he became increasingly interested in providing an entirely new understanding of social systems. One reason is that action carries connotations to human subjects. When we speak of action, we almost automatically imply that it is a subject who acts. In order to avoid that his sociological theory, in the final analysis, was founded on a notion of subjects, he thought that a shift was required from action to communication as the ultimate unit of social systems. To be sure, the notion of communication might be said to allude even stronger to subjects (who but subjects communicate?), but not in Luhmann's special adaption and reformulation of the concept.

Founding the understanding of the social on a notion of communication is not unique to Luhmann's theory. In fact, this Luhmannian ambition forms part of the so-called linguistic turn in social theory which also includes scholars such as Michel Foucault and Jürgen Habermas, among many others. Yet in Luhmann's case the notion of communication carries a very peculiar meaning which can best be explained by comparing it to the classical understandings he wished to go beyond. Classical models of communication assume that communication unfolds as a relation between a sender and a receiver: communication takes place when ego transmits a message which alter then receives. Luhmann finds this sender–receiver model inadequate for several reasons. Most importantly, he complains, anticipating the aversion toward ontology which would be ever-more pronounced as his work progressed:

> The metaphor of transmission is unusable because it implies too much ontology. It suggests that the sender gives up something that the receiver then acquires. This is already incorrect because the sender does not give up anything in the sense of losing it.
>
> (1995g: 139)

An additional problem is, in Luhmann's eyes, that '[t]he metaphor of transmission locates what is essential about communication in the act of transmission, in the utterance. It directs attention and demands for skilfulness onto the one who makes the utterance' (1995g: 139). This too is an erroneous assumption, Luhmann believes; one cannot simply reduce communication to a matter of utterances. But how then to conceive of communication if not as a transmission of utterances? As an alternative to the sender–receiver model, Luhmann suggests that communication be understood as a triple selection, namely as a selection of information, utterance and understanding.

To understand this notion of communication Luhmann begins by reformulating the relation between 'alter' and 'ego'.[7] Specifically, he turns the usual alter–ego relationship around and situates ego as the addressee of communication and alter as the utterer (1995g: 140–1). The first selection appears when alter selects something as information. For example, alter has bought a new beautiful car. This information is now uttered to ego, for instance, in an email. While this would amount to an act of communication according to the classical sender–receiver model, for Luhmann, this still does not constitute communication. The communication is only realised when ego makes the third selection, that of understanding, and this understanding appears when ego is able to observe the information and the act of utterance as separate selections. That is, ego must be able to observe a difference between information and utterance. In Luhmann's own words,

> By understanding, communication grasps a difference between the information value of its content and the reasons for which the content is being uttered. It can thereby accentuate one side or the other and thus pay more attention to the information itself or to the expressive behavior. It is, however, always dependent on experiencing both sides as selection and *thereby* distinguishing them.
>
> (Luhmann 2002e: 157, italics in original)

In the above example, this would mean that ego should be able to observe, for example, that alter's intention with emailing the information about the new car was to invite ego to come and have a ride; or that ego observes that alter is careful not to brag about himself and his new car in that the information is hidden in an email about other issues. The key thing at stake here is to separate communication from perception (Luhmann 2002e: 158). If ego is not able to distinguish between information and utterance, then the two implode into mere noise and no communication emerges. Hearing alter speak in the corridor only becomes communication if ego can observe a difference between information and utterance, i.e. between what is said and the intentions for why/how it is said. If this distinction cannot be established, the noise is only registered as perception.

Crucially, the distinction between information and utterance implies that understanding is a selection which opens up for different ways to proceed (following the various accentuations, see the quote above). Or as Luhmann prefers to speak of it, understanding allows for different ways of *connectivity* and thereby different ways to carry on the autopoiesis of the system. The notion of selectivity also refers to another central point. There is no guarantee that ego has understood alter correctly. There is, in other words, no assurance that ego's understanding of alter's reasons for uttering the information is accurate. It might be, for instance, that the email saying that alter had bought a beautiful new car was meant as irony (alter in fact believes the car is pretty ugly but he could not afford a nicer model). It is also possible that ego misunderstood the information; he misread the email which said 'borrowed' rather than 'bought'.

From the point of view of the autopoiesis of social systems, such misunderstanding does not matter. It can be precisely as productive for creating further communication as would a more factually correct understanding. Furthermore, the connecting communication always 'tests whether the preceding communication was understood. […] The test can turn out negative, and then it often provides an occasion for reflexive communication about communication' (Luhmann 1995g: 143). For example, when ego responds to alter's email, it becomes clear whether the message was understood or if further communication is needed to make clear that alter did in fact invite ego for a ride.

Although communication as such is a triple selection of information, utterance and understanding, every communication gives rise to *a fourth selection* which in itself lies beyond the communication. This fourth selection concerns 'the acceptance or rejection of the specific meaning that was communicated' (Luhmann 1995g: 147). Luhmann's point is that every communication produces a change, however tiny, in ego. Whatever is communicated, ego cannot help being affected in some way by the communication. For example, when ego reads that alter has bought a new car, he might be eager to see it, or he might be envious and try to ignore the message. According to Luhmann, the change that the communication effects in ego works 'like a constraint: it excludes indeterminate arbitrariness in what is now still possible' (1995g: 148). In other words, it establishes the expectation that ego in fact responds within the field of possibilities laid out by the specific communication. Would he like a ride in the car or not? Leaving this open for ego to decide is obviously risky for alter, but this is a risk that no communication can evade: the fourth selection lies entirely with ego; it is he or she who decides whether and how to connect to the communication. As Luhmann puts it in more general terms, the constraint enacted by communication 'always makes resistance possible, and one can know this and take it into consideration before one decides to communicate' (1995g: 148).

It follows from this that Luhmann's notion of communication does not entail consensus or agreement. According to Luhmann, communication neither aims at, nor does it guarantee consensus. This is emphasised as an explicit critique of the work of Habermas which holds that communication implies certain validity claims and that, ideally, one should strive for consensus. Contrary to this position, Luhmann argues that:

> One can also communicate in order to mark dissent, one can desire to argue; and there is no compelling reason to hold the search for consensus to be more rational than the search for dissent. That depends entirely on themes and partners. Communication is

obviously impossible without any consensus, but is also impossible without any dissent.

(2002e: 162)

This argument against Habermas is based on both empirical and normative grounds. Empirically, the lack of consensus is no barrier to the social system's autopoietic self-reproduction. In fact, one might fear that total consensus would be the end to communication. What to communicate about when consensus has been achieved? This touches upon Luhmann's normative reasons for contesting Habermas' consensus ideals. Thus, from a Luhmannian point of view, society can only exist if communication continues to go on. Hence to strive for consensus threatens the vitality, as it were, of society.

Luhmann's redefinition of communication as a triple selection is not the only novelty that his theory presents. He goes on to revolutionise the idea of who communicates. While ordinary conceptions suggest that it is individual subjects who communicate, Luhmann's aversion to the subject-theoretical tradition leads him to propose the radical thesis that *only communication can communicate* (see e.g. Luhmann 2002e: 156). This thesis is related to and substantiated by Luhmann's idea of self-referential, autopoietic systems as well as his strict separation between psychic and social systems. It has already been stated several times that, for Luhmann, social systems are defined by having communication as their fundamental unit of operation. Since social systems are self-referential, autopoietic systems, they continuously produce and reproduce communication and have nothing but their own building blocks, communication, to rely on to enact this self-reproduction. This means that the thoughts of psychic systems remain external to communication. What goes on in the consciousness is not something that enters communication. Whatever students might think while letting their thoughts drift during a boring lecture is not part of the communication that takes place in the classroom. Yet, boredom might be a theme of communication if the teacher observes that students yawn. But even then it is not the students and the teacher that communicate, but rather communication itself. Teacher and students are merely prerequisites for the autopoietic organisation of communication. To avoid any misunderstandings, here as elsewhere Luhmann's notion of communication does not necessarily refer to verbal language, as when the teacher and a student discuss a topic in class. Communication can be non-verbal. A student reading a newspaper or checking emails while the teacher lectures may well be communication.

I mentioned earlier that Luhmann's notion of understanding is conceived partly as a critique of previous action theories in sociology.

Turning to communication is a way for Luhmann to escape this tradition. In the light of this positioning, it is all the more interesting to observe that action actually pops up in Luhmann's theory on a very crucial place. In one of his most thorough discussions of the relation between communication and action, he maintains that from a theoretical viewpoint 'communication cannot be conceived as action, nor can the process of communication be conceived as a chain of actions' (1995g: 164). Communication for Luhmann remains a triple selection, it is not simply a matter of acts of utterance that follow one another. However, and this is the interesting addition, Luhmann states that *communication cannot be observed directly, only inferred. To be observed or to observe itself, a communication system must be flagged as an action system'* (1995g: 164, italics in original). In other words, Luhmann indicates that communication itself is invisible and only enjoys connectivity if it describes itself in action terms. What Luhmann tries to get at here is that communication is only possible if it so to speak tricks itself into believing that it is an action system.

A related problem is, according to Luhmann, that in principle '[c]ommunication is symmetrical insofar as every selection can lead to another and this relationship can be constantly reversed' (1995g: 165). Yet, symmetry is no goal for Luhmann; as with consensus, symmetry does not suggest any direction for future events. Quite the contrary, perfect symmetry leaves anything completely open. In order to reduce complexity, asymmetry is crucial. This leads to the solution Luhmann observes for communication: *'Only by building the understanding of action into a communicative occurrence can communication become asymmetrical*; only thus can a person who utters information give directives to its receiver' (1995g: 165, italics in original). That is, communication must conceal the principal symmetry of its triple selection and begin to observe the utterance as an action. This leads to the following somewhat surprising conclusion:

> Thus, a social system is constituted as an action system on the basis of communicative happenings, and using their operative means. The system generates a description of itself in itself to steer the continuation of the process, the reproduction of the system. Communication's symmetry is made asymmetrical to allow self-observation and self-description […] *And in this abbreviated, simplified, and thereby more easily comprehensible self-description, action – not communication – serves as the final element.*[8]
>
> (Luhmann 1995g: 165, italics added)

As mentioned in the discussion of action and experience, when Luhmann speaks of action he refers to a specific kind of *attribution*, namely selections that are attributed to the system. It follows from this that action is always a communicative trick; the selection is *observed by the social system* to be either action or experience. Hence in Luhmann's view the above quote's reference to action as being the final element of social systems only apparently contradicts the assumption that communication is the final unity of social systems. As he conceives it, the reference to action is merely a way for social systems to make themselves easier to connect to. Be that as it may, it is nevertheless odd to find such a theoretical construction in Luhmann's work, for it resembles the classical distinction between being and appearance which is associated with the Marxist tradition and which Luhmann was careful to distinguish himself from (e.g. Luhmann 1994d).

## THE RELATIONS BETWEEN SOCIAL AND PSYCHIC SYSTEMS

Luhmann's radical proposal that only communication communicates implies a sharp distinction between psychic and social systems. While this distinction has been touched upon in the preceding sections, it merits a more thorough discussion. To begin with, according to Luhmann, psychic systems are self-referential autopoietic systems; their basic elements are consciousness and they are therefore reproduced when operations of consciousness connect to other operations of consciousness. Psychic systems constitute one another's environment, but they also belong to the environment of social systems. It is not possible for one psychic system's operations of consciousness suddenly to interfere in another psychic system's operational modus. If A and B sit in their homes, A's thoughts cannot all of a sudden appear in the brain of B (Luhmann is not a great believer in telepathy). Likewise, the operations of consciousness cannot form part of communication; these operations simply belong to different systemic realms that retain their boundaries and operational closure as long as they exist, Luhmann contends. Although the operational closure of psychic and social systems means that their operations cannot interfere directly in one another, these two types of systems are nevertheless closely affiliated, states Luhmann. One close relation concerns their common medium (meaning); another how they are coupled to one another (interpenetration).

### Interpenetration

Beginning with the latter link, it has been demonstrated above that Luhmann argues that even if no autopoietic system can determine another autopoietic system's operations (otherwise they would not be autopoietic), some systems depend on other systems. This is what the notions of materiality continuum and structural couplings point to. For example, social systems would not be able to operate autopoietically if there were no living systems and no psychic systems in their environment. But there is more at stake than a mere materiality continuum when discussing psychic and social systems. Also, the relation between psychic and social systems is not simply a structural coupling. It is a very particular kind of structural coupling. Thus, argues Luhmann, social and psychic systems develop in a specific 'co-evolutionary' manner where none of them would be able to exist and evolve without the other (Luhmann 1997a: 108). Luhmann applies the (Parsons-derived) notion of *interpenetration* to account for this co-constitutive relationship. Interpenetration describes specific inter-system relations and should be distinguished from what Luhmann calls penetration:

> We speak of "penetration" if a system *makes* its own *complexity* (and with it indeterminacy, contingency, and the pressure to select) *available for constructing another system*. Precisely in this sense social systems presuppose "life." Accordingly, *interpenetration* exists when this occurs reciprocally, that is, when both systems enable each other by introducing their own already-constituted complexity into each other.
>
> (Luhmann 1995g: 213, italics in original)

So while penetration points to the materiality continuum which is needed for systems to exist, interpenetration describes occasions where this materiality continuum is reciprocally constituted, and where the systems rely on the complexity they make available for one another. For example, social systems cannot exist without life in their environment, but this dependence is not mutual. Cells and immune systems may work perfectly well without the complexities that social systems make available. For social and psychic systems this is different; they presuppose the complexities of each other. Thus, social systems cannot develop without the complexities that thoughts provide, just as psychic systems can only evolve on condition that they are stimulated by communication. To illustrate, a refinement of thinking often goes hand in hand with a refinement of communication: thoughts on quantum physics depend on specialised scientific communication on the topic.

To be sure, Luhmann recognises, there is a slight asymmetry at stake here. For whereas it is possible for consciousness to bracket out for a moment the influence of communication and operate independently of communicative stimulation (one can sit alone at a bench and gaze at the sea for several hours, letting one thought lead to the next), the opposite is not possible for social systems. This is due to psychic systems' particular ability to *perceive*, an ability that serves as a crucial continuous stimulus for social systems, although the latter operate through communications rather than perceptions. Luhmann describes this communicative reliance on the perceptions of the psychic system as follows:

> Remarkable is the fact that communication can be stimulated only by the mind and not by physical, chemical, biochemical, or neuro-physiological operations as such. Radioactivity, smog, and diseases of all sorts may increase or decrease. Such a fact can have no effect on communication if it is not perceived, measured, and made conscious; only then can the fact stimulate the attempt to communicate about it according to the rules of communication. Even in an airplane that is about to crash, it becomes possible to communicate about the impending crash only if it is perceived. The crash itself cannot influence communication; it can only end it.
>
> (2002f: 177)

As this quote suggests, Luhmann sees communication as something that is triggered by the perception of the mind. The consciousness perceives something and is affected in a way which propels the social system to select an information and thereby begin establishing communication as a triple selection. According to the principle of autopoiesis, however, the perception of the mind only irritates social systems; it does not intrude their operational reproduction. To repeat this general point once again: every system is only able to irritate other systems, meaning that interpenetration is also only about making complexity available for one another (as when scientific communication makes its complexity available for thoughts on quantum physics); it is not about substituting or intervening directly in other systems' operations.

## Meaning

Given Luhmann's insistence that autopoietic systems do not have the capacity to penetrate one another in the sense of infiltrating each other with their operations, one may argue that the notions of penetration and interpenetration are not particularly well-chosen. After all, these notions clearly connote intrusion and the collapse of strict system/environment boundaries. Be that as it may, I do not want to enter a discussion of the terminological appropriateness here, but would like instead to turn to the other phenomenon that links psychic and social systems, namely their common medium of *meaning*. In continuation of the points made above, Luhmann writes:

Psychic and social systems have evolved together. [...] This co-evolution has led to a common achievement, employed by psychic as well as social systems. Both kinds of systems are ordered according to it, and for both it is binding as the indispensable, undeniable form of their complexity and self-reference. We call this evolutionary achievement "meaning."

(1995g: 58)

Luhmann's interest in meaning dates back to his earliest writings. Thus, the discussion book with Habermas contained an important chapter where Luhmann argued for seeing 'Meaning as Sociology's Basic Concept' (Luhmann 1990k). Luhmann's sociological understanding of the concept was derived from his reading and adaptation of Edmund Husserl's phenomenology. The Husserlian reference is clear when Luhmann describes meaning as related to intentionality and a horizon of possibilities:

The phenomenon of meaning appears as a surplus of references to other possibilities of experience and action. Something stands in the focal point, at the center of intention, and all else is indicated marginally as the horizon of an "and so forth" of experience and action. In this form, everything that is intended holds open to itself the world as a whole, thus guaranteeing the actuality of the world in the form of accessibility.

(1995g: 60)

In spite of the phenomenological underpinnings, Luhmann is careful to stress how his view on meaning differs from classical phenomenological accounts. Most importantly, Luhmann does not accept Husserl's ambition to found meaning in a transcendental subject, nor does he see intention seen as *subjective* intention. For Luhmann, meaning must be 'defined without reference to the concept of subject' (e.g. Luhmann 1990k: 23).[9] Instead, meaning is conceived by Luhmann as the medium through which both psychic and social systems reproduce themselves. Psychic and social systems are simply unthinkable without meaning.

What is it that meaning does for these systems? To answer this question one might begin by noting what is intimated in the quote above: meaning is 'not something substantial or phenomenal' (2002a: 229), but refers instead to a specific medium that operates with *the distinction between the actual and the possible*. Meaning points to the potentiality (the horizon) of selections other than the one which is presently actualised. At the same time, there is an intentionality inherent in meaning. Communication is only possible as communication *about something*; just as thoughts in the psychic system are always thoughts *about something* (Kneer and Nassehi 1993: 76). But whatever is intended and selected, it always implicitly refers to the horizon of (yet) un-actualised potentials, and this applies as well to any connecting selections. At one gathering, for example, the wine enthusiasts may discuss nothing but the quality of pinot noir grapes; and the actualisation of this topic appears on the backcloth of all the other grapes that could also have been debated. This constant play between the actual and the potential endows meaning with an inherent instability, but also with a particular temporal structure:

> Meaning is the continual actualization of potentialities. But because meaning can be meaning only as the difference between what is actual at any moment and a horizon of possibilities, every actualization also leads to a virtualization of the potentialities that could be connected up with it. The instability of meaning resides in the untenability of its core of actuality [...] Thus one can treat the difference between actuality and possibility in terms of temporal displacement and thereby process indications of possibility with every (new) actuality.
>
> (Luhmann 1995g: 65)

Interestingly, the notion of meaning is closely related to a number of Luhmann's other key concepts. For example, the relation between the actual and the potential corresponds to that between complexity and the need for complexity reduction. The world is characterised by enormous complexity (potentiality) which calls for complexity reduction (actualisation). Relatedly, meaning and contingency are intimately associated terms. Contingency refers to the fact that everything could be different, and precisely this is also conveyed by the notion of meaning. This is further emphasised by the functional method which utilises this contingency as a systematic approach to examine in more detail how problems and solutions could be related in other (potential) ways than the ones currently actualised. Last but not least the incessant 're-actualization and re-virtualization' of meaning amounts to a continuous reproduction of the meaning systems; indeed, Luhmann states, this 'auto-agility of meaning occurrences is autopoiesis par excellence' (1995g: 65, 66).

## Meaning decomposed: The fact, temporal and social meaning dimensions

It might be argued that, although meaning refers to the distinction between the actual and the potential, it remains a rather broad category. Thus, one might critically ask, is meaning interesting as anything but a general medium that is claimed to be constitutive for psychic and social systems? Is it, in other words, possible to derive some analytical implications of the concept, or should one simply accept meaning as a basic given in Luhmann's theory? Luhmann is aware that meaning as such is a rather abstract concept and he therefore adds flesh to it by arguing that it can be decomposed into three so-called meaning dimensions. These are the fact dimension, the temporal dimension and the social dimension.

The *fact dimension* operates with a distinction between 'this' and 'something else' (1995g: 76). Any meaning, whether it is thought or communicated, can be analysed according to whether it refers to 'this' theme or fact, or to 'something else'. Whatever is pointed out as 'this' implicitly refers to the horizon of 'something else'. Is the communication in question about wine or punk music? And if it is about wine, is it then concerned with wine production or wine consumption, with Italian or Chilean wines, etc.? While the fact dimension separates between 'this' and 'something else', the *temporal meaning dimension* revolves around the distinction between 'before' and 'after'. In the temporal dimension, everything is 'ordered only according to the when and not to the who/what/where/how of experience and action' (1995g: 78). For example, the temporal meaning dimension is actualised if the wine enthusiasts discuss the best years of wine production in France. Finally, the *social dimension* is concerned with the distinction between alter and ego. More specifically, it 'means that one can ask of every meaning whether another experiences it in exactly the same way I do' (Luhmann 1995g: 80). Whatever ego does or experiences can be reflected upon by ego with respect to what alter might have done or experienced. The possible differences, leading also to discussions of consensus and dissent, are thematised by the social meaning dimension.

The three meaning dimensions can be seen as analytical tools which open up for the study of specific communications and allow for more substantial analyses of how meaning is produced and reproduced. Thus, communication can be studied according to how it actualises and combines the three meaning dimensions. How, in brief, do specific communications address the questions of what (fact), when (temporal) and who (social)? To illustrate, political discussions about how to deal with climate change can be examined according to all three meaning dimensions. The fact dimension is addressed in deliberations about what initiatives are best; should focus be on global carbon markets or on legal measures? The temporal dimension is activated in discussions about what year should be the benchmark for considering future reductions. Should it be 2000 or 2005, and by when should the reductions be actualised? Finally, the social dimension is referred to in discussions about who should pay for the measures and their consequences? Should the bill be send to the developed countries, and who among these should carry the heaviest burdens?

While the decomposition of meaning into the three meaning dimensions clearly opens up analytical perspectives not contained by the abstract notion of meaning, it also gives rise to new critical inquiries. For how can it be that Luhmann arrives at precisely these three meaning dimensions and not others? Why, for example, does space not figure as a separate meaning dimension? This question has been discussed by the prominent systems theorist Rudolf Stichweh who took over Luhmann's professorship when the latter retired. According to Stichweh, an authority on Luhmann's work, there is no obvious theoretical reason why Luhmann elevated time and not (also) space to being a meaning dimension (Stichweh 1998: 344). Interestingly, Luhmann hardly elucidates why he focuses on the fact, temporal and social dimensions of meaning. To be sure, in the article on meaning as sociology's basic concept, Luhmann refers to the work of the Polish philosopher Adam Schaff as a source of inspiration for separating between fact, temporal and social meaning dimensions, all of which can be located in Schaff's work (Luhmann 1990k: 72, n. 23; Schaff 1962). While this may be an inspirational backdrop, it still does not really explain why exactly *these* dimensions.

Arguably an answer to this question appears in the introduction to the book on power that Luhmann published in 1975. Here he states that the kind of theory of society that he seeks to develop must contain and build upon three layers: one is a theory of differentiation; the next is a theory of evolution; and the third is a theory of symbolically generalised media of communication (1979: 108). Interestingly, these theoretical complexes address each of the three meaning dimensions. Thus, the theory of societal differentiation is concerned with a differentiation of ever new factual horizons, for example, the differentiation of systems of economy, law, science, politics, art, etc. The theory of evolution corresponds to the interest in the temporal dimension. Finally, as I shall come back to in Chapter 4, the theory of symbolically generalised media of communication is an attempt to understand how ego and alter relate to each other's uncertainty about what the other might think and do; hence, this theoretical layer is concerned in essence with the social meaning dimension. To summarise, it seems reasonable to assume that the reason why Luhmann operates with the fact dimension, the temporal dimension and the social dimension as the specific meaning dimensions is that this produces a theory-internal resemblance of his wish to found sociology on a combined theory of differentiation, evolution and symbolically generalised media of communication. While this is at least an explanation, the question then is if it is an adequate justification of Luhmann's decision to operate with only three meaning dimensions. Again, could it not be argued that a theory of society would also have to account for spatial differences, which would speak in favour of treating space as a separate meaning dimension?

## THE INDIVIDUAL REVISITED

In continuation of the discussion of how psychic and social systems are related, it is now time to deal more fully with Luhmann's view on the sociological status of humans. Luhmann revolts against the 'anthropocentric' stance of much sociology – Weber, rational choice, Goffman, etc. – which places the individual subject at the centre of attention (King and Thornhill 2003: 2). Luhmann is highly critical of such theories which, perhaps unintentionally, situate the human subject at their base. His reservations are theoretical, as he finds it misleading to ground a theory of society on human subjects. But his reservations are also based on historical arguments:

> there have been so many dreadful experiences with 'human creators' that one prefers to warn against them. Far too often ideas about the human have served to cement role asymmetries by means of external references and so as to withdraw their social disposition. Here one may think of race ideologies, of the distinction between the chosen and the condemned, of what the socialist doctrines prescribed, or of what was suggested by the melting pot ideology and the American way of life of the North Americans. None of this inspires repetition or even new modified attempts; indeed, *all experiences speak in favour of theories that save us from humanisms*.
>
> (1994a: 55–6, italics added)

This is one of the rare moments where Luhmann unleashes his normative position in very explicit terms: the reason we should be sceptical about theories that revolve around human subjects is that they easily lend themselves to ideological misuse. That is, they easily lead to suggestions for the 'improvement' of humans, with all the terrifying prospects that entails. Luhmann is therefore happy to adopt an explicitly 'antihumanist' stance (Luhmann 1997a: 35).[10]

More specifically, this antihumanist position suggests that humans are not part of society, but belong to its environment.[11] At first sight this statement appears wholly unacceptable. How can humans not be part of society? Does this not contradict any everyday experience? On closer inspection, the idea of leaving out humans of society follows as a radical implication of the assertion that the social is constituted by communication. If society is the name for the totality of communication, i.e. of social systems, and if only communication can communicate, then humans must necessarily be exterior to society. Indeed, argues Luhmann, rather than being part of society (and rather than being a unity), a human being is in fact a conglomerate of various autopoietic systems: a psychic system as well as several living systems (cells, immune system, etc.). Strictly speaking, therefore, a human being cannot be part of society. There is no way that the operationally closed system of communication can integrate operations from the psychic system or from the various parts of the organism. According to Luhmann, theories that ignore this operational logic and fail to distinguish between social systems of communication, on the one hand, and human beings as systemic conglomerations, on the other, operate with a too simplified notion of individuals. 'In fact,' he states, reversing the accusation – advanced in (mis)readings such as Mingers (2008) – that his systems theory must be deflected for its antihumanist stance, 'the theory of autopoietic systems could bear the title *Taking Individuals Seriously*, certainly more seriously than our humanistic tradition' (Luhmann 1992b: 1422, italics in original).

The exclusion of human beings from society does not mean that Luhmann has nothing more substantial to say about humans than that they constitute bodily containers of systemic conglomerations. For example, it follows from the notions of structural couplings, interdependence and materiality continuum that, even if humans are not part of society, there would be no society if there were no humans (this is ignored in the critique advanced by Mingers 2008). Communication would not exist without the presence of psychic and living systems. But Luhmann goes further than this. Most importantly, in several analyses he places the notions of 'persons' and 'individuality' centrally and seeks to account for how humans are made relevant in social systems. This includes historical investigations as well as conceptual inventions. On the conceptual-theoretical side, Luhmann argues for studying persons and individuality on the basis of a distinction between inclusion and exclusion:

> Inclusion (and respectively exclusion) can only refer to the way that humans are *indicated*, i.e., made relevant, in communication. Following the traditional meaning of the term ['persons', CB] one might say that inclusion and exclusion refer to how humans are treated as 'persons'.
>
> (Luhmann 1995d: 241, italics in original)

The notion of indication will be explained in Chapter 3. For now the important point is that '[p]ersons are not systems, but rather points of identification in the communication' (Kneer and Nassehi 1993: 87). That is, 'persons' is the name that systems theory employs to describe how humans are *addressed in communication* (or in the thoughts of psychic systems). When the groups of punks communicate about Sid Vicious from the Sex Pistols, he as a human being is not part of the communication, but he is addressed in it and therefore appears as a person in systems-theory terms. One might argue that just as communication tricks itself into believing that it is an action system, so communication evades its fundamental exclusion of humans by constructing persons as themes or even partners of communication. Yet persons are more than a mere trick. Thus, Luhmann says, 'a person is constituted for the sake of ordering behavioral expectations that can be fulfilled by him or her' (1995g: 315). In other words, the notion of persons refers to expectations that structure communication. Being addressed as a punk, for instance, means being seen as a person to whom certain expectations are attributed (taste of music, clothing, attitudes, etc.). Obviously, the same human being can constitute several persons according to the communicative context (the kind of inclusion at stake). In one context he or she may be addressed as a parent, in another as a politician, in a third as a religious believer. This might seem to bear some resemblance to the more standard sociological concept of roles, but persons and roles should not be conflated, states Luhmann (1995g: 315–7). The former refers to specific human beings, whereas the latter describes a more general layer of expectations that can be performed by many different human beings. For example, a president of a country refers to a specific role with specific expectations associated with it. But when we speak of Mr. Obama we address him as a person.

In addition to this conceptual discussion, Luhmann examines individuality from a more historical point of view in his semantic studies. As mentioned in Chapter 1, in this part of his work, Luhmann investigates how a society's semantics, i.e. its conceptual store or apparatus, is related to its structure. This societal structure does not refer to the economic basis of society, as Marxism would have it, but rather to society's primary mode of differentiation. Luhmann distinguishes between three main forms of societal differentiation (see also Figure 2.4 below). The most basic form is named *segmentary differentiation*. This refers to a society which is based on minor segmentary units such as clans and tribes that provide the included individuals with all their needs. This form of organisation is usually associated with traditional societies and knows no form of division of labour or functional differentiation between the segments. More developed forms of society cultivate a *stratificatory* or hierarchical mode of differentiation. Here, society is

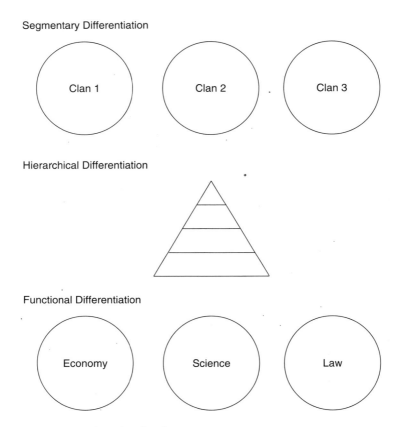

*Figure 2.4* Societal Modes of Differentiation.

differentiated according to different strata; some are conceived as being above others. This kind of differentiation is known from European societies in the Middle Ages, or from the caste society of India. Finally, Luhmann argues that, at least in a European context, the hierarchically differentiated societies were replaced by a new primary mode of differentiation, which was completed in the eighteenth and nineteenth centuries, namely *functional differentiation*, i.e. a differentiation of society into a number of operationally autonomous function systems (law, science, politics, religion, art, etc.).[12] The transition amounts, for Luhmann, to a transition from pre–modern to modern society.

Luhmann relates these modes of differentiation to the question of individuality. Specifically, he argues that in both segmentary and hierarchically differentiated societies, an individual only acquires status through his or her inclusion in specific segments or strata. In a hierarchically differentiated society, for example, belonging to the strata of nobility defines how the person is addressed as well as what specific expectations and opportunities this social position entails. Crucially, moreover, in both segmentary and hierarchically differentiated societies, each person is included in only one system. One cannot be a member of two tribes at a · time, just as one cannot be part of two strata simultaneously (Luhmann 1995d: 242–4). According to Luhmann, this changes fundamentally when functional differentiation takes over as the primary mode of societal differentiation. First of all, no functional system can provide a full inclusion of an individual. No person is only, say, a scientist or an artist. Everybody constantly fluctuates between inclusions in various functional systems (then in the economic system when paying for a beer in a bar; then in the system of religion when praying to God; then in the political system when debating political initiatives; etc.). This also means that nobody can define his or her individuality on basis of the inclusion, as this constantly changes from one context to the next. Accordingly, argues Luhmann, a new form of individuality emerges in the modern, functionally differentiated society, namely an 'exclusion individuality' (Luhmann 1989b: 160).

This exclusion individuality might be interpreted as a simultaneous burden and emancipation of the modern individual. On the one hand, the individual can no longer rely on specific systems in the definition of his or her individuality; the individual must be constructed independently of these systems, on their outside or as their residue, so to speak. Bluntly put, one's identity is no longer defined by birth; rather it is something that requires constant work. While this can be seen as a burden, it may on the other hand be seen as a liberation from narrowing social structures. The functional differentiation lends the individual more space to carve out his or her specific individuality. Referring to Durkheim, Luhmann describes this as a 'relation of intensification' [*Steigerungsverhältnis*] (1995b: 130). Increasing societal differentiation does not lead to less individuality. Quite the contrary, there is more room for individuality the more differentiated society is.

# 3

# Observing systems

Ever since Luhmann published *Social Systems* his work has been associated with the notion of autopoiesis. The 'autopoietic turn' not only had obvious sociological implications for how to conceive of social systems. Luhmann was also interested in the epistemological implications that followed from the new foundation he wanted to give sociology. This interest was visible already in *Social Systems*, the final chapter of which was concerned with 'consequences for epistemology' (1995g: Ch. 12). While this chapter was very brief and could only unpack the implications in a very sketchy manner, the subsequent years showed that Luhmann became increasingly occupied with epistemological issues. Indeed, as mentioned in Chapter 1, I think it is warranted to speak of a third phase in Luhmann's work which really set off in the late 1980s and which revolved around notions such as observation, distinction, re-entry and paradoxes.

Luhmann's epistemological considerations are founded on this conceptual apparatus. If the notion of autopoiesis was unfamiliar to sociological thinking prior to Luhmann, then the entire vocabulary of observation, re-entries, etc. is no less foreign. It does not help that Luhmann's understanding of these concepts are derived from his reading of a virtually unknown and 'obscure mathematician' (Knodt 1995: xi), George Spencer-Brown and his book *Laws of Form* (1969). The aim of the present chapter is to explain the content and sociological value of the concepts of observation, distinction, etc. This will include a discussion of Spencer-Brown's little-known work.

It is important to note, and this will also be demonstrated below, that although Luhmann's interest in these concepts stems from his wish to account for the epistemological foundation and implications of the autopoietic turn, the epistemological elaborations in fact results in a reformulation of his sociological theory (which is the reason why it makes sense to categorise his late work as an independent phase). Specifically, he argues for the need for turning sociology into a science that studies social phenomena on the basis of so-called second-order observations, i.e. observations of observations. So the autopoietic turn leads to epistemological reflections which ultimately re-directs Luhmann's sociological interests and actually gives autopoiesis a less dominant role in the theoretical architecture.

## DRAW A DISTINCTION!

I will begin my discussion of Luhmann's third phase by examining George Spencer-Brown's *Laws of Form* since, from the late 1980s onward, this book occupies a most crucial place in almost all of Luhmann's writings. Indeed, Luhmann's later work is heavily infused with vocabulary from and references to this around 150 pages long treatise. As a result of Luhmann's almost fanatic wish to foreground Spencer-Brownian terms, several critical analyses of Luhmann have pivoted around discussions of Spencer-Brown. For example, Rodrigo Jokisch has argued that Luhmann's later work is based so much on *Laws of Form* that critique aimed at Spencer-Brown will automatically target Luhmann as well (Jokisch 1996: 66).[1] While for some commentators Spencer-Brown thus becomes Luhmann's Achilles heel, any comparison of the work of the two readily reveals major differences. Luhmann is certainly inspired by Spencer-Brown's treatise, but he only adopts those ideas from Spencer-Brown that he can utilise sociologically. There is accordingly a great contrast between many of the logical and mathematical ideas and calculations put forward in *Laws of Form* and the rather few concepts that reappear in Luhmann's sociology.

What, then, is this mathematical treatise all about? According to Spencer-Brown, '[t]he theme of this book is that a universe comes into being when a space is severed or taken apart' (1969: v). Spencer-Brown's ambitious aim is, on basis of this idea, to 'reconstruct, with an accuracy and coverage that appear almost uncanny, the basic forms underlying linguistic, mathematical, physical, and biological science', so as to 'see how familiar laws of our own experience follow inexorably from the original act of severance' (1969: v). Compared to this highly ambitious objective, Luhmann adoption of Spencer-Brownian ideas is more modest and restricted to the sociological and epistemological consequences he can derive from *Laws of Form*. This revolves not least around Spencer-Brown's understanding of distinction and form. '[A] distinction is drawn by arranging a boundary with separate sides so that a point on one side cannot reach the other side without crossing the boundary', states Spencer-Brown (1969: 1). This can easily be interpreted in Luhmannian terms: the system/environment distinction establishes a boundary with strictly separated sides. Similar to Luhmann, moreover, Spencer-Brown's treatise is triggered by the introduction of a distinction. 'Draw a distinction', reads the injunction that sets off the mathematical calculus in *Laws of Form* (1969: 3). When the first distinction is drawn, the work can begin. And '[o]nce a distinction is drawn, the spaces, states, or contents on each side of the boundary, being distinct, can be indicated' (1969: 1). Spencer-Brown invents the following symbol to express 'a mark of distinction': ⌐ (1969: 4). There is an inbuilt asymmetry in this symbol, in that it signifies that the inner (rather than the outer) side of the distinction is indicated. Following this way of symbolising distinctions, Luhmann's main distinction can be expressed as follows: system̄ environment.

The notions of distinction and indication are combined in Luhmann's definition of observation. '*Observing* can be defined as an operation using a distinction for indicating one side of the distinction and not the other' (Luhmann 1993c: 485, italics in original). For example, when I look at my book shelves and observe a book written by Flaubert, this observation is a double operation where I first distinguish the Flaubert book from the other books, and then indicate the Flaubert side of the distinction.[2] Or to be more precise, according to Luhmann, this two-step procedure is actually carried out in only one step. If the distinction and indication did not occur simultaneously, observation would not be one operation, but rather two operations.

There are three important implications of this understanding of observation. First, if there is no distinction, there can be no indication. The latter simply presupposes the former. I cannot indicate the Flaubert side of the distinction without separating it from something which it is not. Second, it follows from this that every distinction is a 'two-sided distinction' (Luhmann 2000a: 65). Every observation always carries with it the side of the distinction which is not (presently) indicated. This is also the message conveyed by Spencer-Brown's definition of form: 'Call the space cloven by any distinction, together with the entire content of the space, the form of the distinction' (1969: 4). So form, for Luhmann and Spencer-Brown, does not refer to the shape of some object, for example, the form or shape of a coffee pot or a Flaubert book. Contrary to this everyday understanding, Luhmann's and Spencer-Brown's notion of form always includes the side of the distinction which is not (currently) indicated. The *form is the unity of the difference* between the two sides; so the distinction's two sides are always given simultaneously, although only one side can be indicated at a time. This again goes hand in hand with Luhmann's emphasis on every system's reliance on its environment. It makes no sense for Luhmann to speak of a system without at the same time, though perhaps implicitly, assuming that it is distinguished from an environment.

Spencer-Brown uses the notions of marked and unmarked state to describe what side of a distinction is indicated at any given moment. The marked state is the indicated side; the unmarked is the non-indicated side (Spencer-Brown 1969: 4,5). I will employ this vocabulary to discuss the third important implication of Luhmann's notion of observation. As Niels Åkerstrøm Andersen has argued, Luhmann's interest in how systems observe through distinctions thus opens up for an analytical approach which constantly asks what is at the excluded side, the unmarked side, which together with the marked side constitutes the unity of the distinction (Andersen 2003: 78–80). When, for example, I observe my Flaubert book, what distinction do I actually employ? Do I distinguish between the Flaubert book and all my other books? Or do I distinguish more specifically between the Flaubert book and a book by, say, Don DeLillo? Since the unmarked state is usually only given implicitly, the sociologist may try to explicate the unmarked side which is constitutive for the observation. Andersen gives the name 'form analysis' to this Luhmann-inspired strategy of analysis (Andersen 2003: 78–80). As Andersen points out, such an analysis of the two-sided forms of observation might reveal that what appears to be the same observation in fact refers to different forms and thus have different meanings. For example, if people speak of 'safety', the unmarked state may differ markedly, implying that entirely different content is attributed to 'safety'. For a victim of rape, the unmarked side of safety might be 'sexual assault'. For an orphan after the earthquake in Haiti, the unmarked side of safety might be 'living in the street'. And for a middle-class European, the unmarked side of safety might be 'expensive healthcare'. The point is that here the same word, 'safety', refers to three very different forms, and therefore carries very different meanings.[3]

### Re-entries and paradoxes

Having defined what constitutes the form of distinctions, Spencer-Brown goes on to develop a complex calculus that has both arithmetic and algebraic parts. Here Spencer-Brown uses the mark of distinction, ⌐, as the means through which a new mathematical framework is unfolded, based on the binary distinction between two values, namely a marked and an unmarked state. The majority of this part of *Laws of*

*Form* is very technical and will not be explored in the present context. Yet one of his elaborations merits attention, as it plays an important role for Luhmann. At the end of his technical calculations, Spencer-Brown thus enters a difficulty. While his initial arithmetic and algebraic endeavours were based on finite mathematical expressions, where any expression could be broken down into one of two values (marked or unmarked state), the calculus faces a problem when confronted with infinite expressions. It is simply not possible to establish the value of an infinite mathematical expression; whether it can be boiled down to a marked or an unmarked state cannot be determined.

Spencer-Brown now suggests that this challenge can be handled by introducing a new notion, that of *re-entry*, which refers to a form that contains itself (one might compare this to fractals where the whole is mirrored by the parts, see Kauffman 1987: 63–5). Again, the technical aspects of this procedure need not be discussed here. More importantly, the notion of re-entry activates *self-reference*; and self-reference buttresses the problem of indeterminacy. By way of a well-known example from logics, the so-called Liar paradox, one version of which reads 'this sentence is false', illustrates a self-referential form that is characterised by an 'unresolvable indeterminacy' (Spencer-Brown 1969: 57): If the sentence is true, then it is false, and vice versa. No simple solution seems to be at hand. However, argues Spencer-Brown, there is in fact a way out of this self-referential paradox. The solution just has to be found in another dimension, that of *time*. To illustrate this he imagines a circle drawn on a piece a paper. This inner side of the circle represents the marked state of the distinction, whereas its outer side is the unmarked state. Spencer-Brown then adds an imaginary tunnel to this image (Spencer-Brown 1969: 58–60). The tunnel hovers under the paper and connects the inner and the outer sides. Now, if the inner side symbolises 'true' and the outside symbolises 'false', then the Liar paradox amounts to a constant oscillation through the tunnel from one side to the other. As everyone knows, passing through a tunnel takes time. This means that a paradoxical, self-referential form need not obstruct thinking and further processing; rather the paradox is de-paradoxified in time. Time becomes a way to avoid a standstill and enables an analysis of the paradox.

While this might sound rather odd and at any rate irrelevant to sociological theory, Luhmann thinks differently. He applies the notion of re-entry directly to the level of social systems. Indeed, Luhmann argues, re-entry is a highly apt term to describe a wide range of social phenomena. It frequently happens that social systems incorporate the system/environment distinction into the system. For example, such a re-entry of the system/environment distinction into the system side of the system/environment distinction is crucial to any form of reflection and rationality, Luhmann contends. He thus defines systemic *reflection* as the situation where a system observes either the system or the environment side of the re-entered system/environment distinction (Luhmann 1995g: 455). For example, an organisation displays reflection when it considers itself a unity and discusses how to brand itself in a new way. Systemic *rationality* is at stake when the system observes the *unity* of the re-entered system/environment distinction (1995g: 474). For example, an organisation demonstrates systemic rationality if it 'control[s] its effects on the environment by checking their repercussions upon itself' (1995g: 475). In this way, the system observes how its actions affect the unity of the difference between system and environment. The difference between reflection and rationality is shown is Figure 3.1.

## OBSERVING SYSTEMS

Another important sociological implication of the notion of re-entry concerns what Luhmann describes as the fact that distinctions can only be made 'self-implicatively' (1990a: 84). No distinction can be made (and this also applies to the initial distinction that *Laws of Forms* instructs the reader to draw) without already presuming and simultaneously

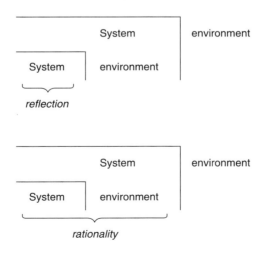

*Figure 3.1* Reflection and Rationality as Based on Re-Entry of the System/Environment Distinction.

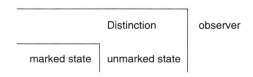

*Figure 3.2* The Distinction and the Observer.

installing a distinction between the distinction and the observer who draws the distinction. That is, when I draw a mark of distinction on paper, I simultaneously draw a distinction between this mark and myself. This means that, on a very fundamental level, any distinction marks a re-entry; the form of distinction always appears as a re-entered form of distinction (see Figure 3.2).

While this might once again sound speculative, it has the important sociological implication that since any distinction entails a re-entry, Luhmann here finds support for his key assertion in *Social Systems*, namely 'that there are systems' (Luhmann 1995g: 12). By emphasising the ever-presence of re-entries, *Laws of Form* in effect shows that distinctions always take place in a network of other distinctions (Baecker 1993: 31–2).

The double reference to the unmarked side of the distinction as well as to the observer drawing the distinction is crucial to Luhmann and forms the basis of his preoccupation with the notion of observation from the late 1980s onward. In his farewell lecture from 1993, he uses this double reference to present an alternative to the sociological perspectives of Marx and Durkheim. According to Luhmann, Durkheim was interested in examining 'what is the case?', whereas Marx focused on 'what lies behind it' (Luhmann 1994d). Contrary to these inquiries, Luhmann follows Spencer-Brown and states: That which lies behind (Marx) when something is the case (Durkheim) is partly that which is not presently indicated (the unmarked state), and partly the observer drawing the distinction (Baecker 1999b: 45; Luhmann 1994d). Consequently, the analytical task of the sociologist becomes, in this programme, to study the observer(s) who observe what the case is and to scrutinise the distinctions (the marked and unmarked states) employed in the observations. In a different formulation, since Luhmann subscribes to a dictum of Maturana that 'everything said is said by an observer', the sociologist should focus on the observer and on how (through which distinctions) the observer observes (Luhmann 1993b: 769).

In order to account analytically for the observer who is 'behind' any distinction, Luhmann draws on the cybernetic work of Heinz von

Foerster (1984a) and provides his sociological theory with a new analytical edifice, namely that of so-called *second-order observation*. While first-order observation refers to *what* an observer observes, second-order observation is concerned with *how* the first-order observer observes.[4] That is, the second-order observer is not so interested in making claims about the world as in the distinctions employed by the first-order observer when he or she makes claims about the world. To illustrate, it is a first-order observation to state that 'the politics proposed by Mr. XX is immoral'. A second-order observation, by contrast, would focus on the distinction used, i.e. that politics is observed here on the basis of a moral distinction.

Luhmann makes clear that every second-order observation is also a first-order observation in the sense that it draws a distinction and indicates one and not the other side.

> But second-order observation is indeed not only first-order observation. It is both more and less. It is less because it observes *only* observers and nothing else. It is more because it not only sees (= distinguishes) its object [the observer, CB] but also sees what the object sees and sees how it sees what it sees, and perhaps even sees what it does not see and sees that it does not see that it does not see what it does not see. On the level of second-order observation, one can thus see everything: what the observed observer sees, and what the observed observer does not see. [...] Only one thing is necessarily excluded: the observation that is actualized in the very moment of observing, its functioning as a first-order observation.
> (Luhmann 2002c: 114–5, italics in original)

Although Foucault would not formulate it as formalistic, a parallel can be identified here to his genealogies of problematisations (Foucault 1997). In Luhmann's vocabulary, Foucault does not make first-order observations about the constitution of the social world, but observes from a second-order perspective how observes have problematised (i.e. observed) various phenomena throughout history. So, for example, Foucault does not claim that the panopticon, famously analysed in *Discipline and Punish*, is in fact an effective way of disciplining subjects (this would be a first-order observation). Rather he is interested in the fact that at a given time in history the panopticon was observed as an efficient power technology (Foucault 1977). Similarly, Luhmann is interested in how observers construct the world: what distinctions do they apply? What is left unmarked in the observations? How does the social world emerge as a play of observing observers?

One of Luhmann's reasons for giving priority to second-order observations is that it offers a way of handling the problem of the *blind spot* which is inherent to any observation (see von Foerster 1984b: 288–9; 1992: 49–51). When somebody draws a distinction and indicates the one and not the other side, it is only the indicated side which is apparent to the observer. The form of the distinction (with its two sides) constitutes a blind spot for the observer. If, for example, it is I who says that Mr. XX proposes an immoral political programme, then this observation is blind to the form of distinction (moral | immoral politics) that I use. In the moment something is observed, the observer is not able to see what form of distinction he or she employs. Yet this first form of distinction may be observed in a new observation, which, however, produces a new blind spot that can only be observed in a new observation, and so on. To illustrate, I may make a new observation to observe how I observed Mr. XX (a second-order observation). This would mean that I observe the form of the distinction I used about Mr. XX. But this new observation is itself blind to the form of distinction it applies in the moment of observation. To put it figuratively, the eye that observes cannot see itself in the act of observation. That is, the blind spot refers to the fact that the observer cannot see that he or she cannot see what he or she cannot see (see the quote above).

Luhmann argues that the emphasis on second rather than first-order observation effects a transition from ontology to epistemology. Instead of making claims about the ontological constitution of the social world (the social *is* this or that), a sociology that devotes itself to second-order observation is concerned entirely with epistemological aspects (*how* do observes observe; *how* do they believe the world is constituted?). Indeed, Luhmann says, ontology only becomes interesting to a second-order observer when this observer observes that other observers operate with ontological distinctions, which happens whenever observations are made on basis of the distinction between being and non-being (e.g. Luhmann 2002c: 116). I will return to the epistemological level when discussing Luhmann's constructivist programme below.

Luhmann's emphasis on second-order observation might be said to produce a slight tension in his work. Although he gives the impression in the last phase of his work that his sociological systems theory follows the mode of second-order observation (which in many cases it clearly does), there are also parts of the theory that may be said to operate on a first-order level. Most significantly, even if the notion of autopoiesis no longer attracts the primary attention of Luhmann in this phase, his understanding of social systems is still based on the autopoietic framework. And this framework amounts, I would claim, to a first-order level: It asserts that there are systems and that these systems do actually operate according to an autopoietic logic. Thus, Luhmann's account of how social systems operate is not founded on second-order observations of how observes observe the operative mode, but is based instead on a theoretical claim of how the social world is constituted.

A final comment on second-order observation is warranted. Since Luhmann's introduction of a second-order level of observation might inspire calls for even higher orders (e.g. third or fourth-order observations), it should be noted that Luhmann sees no reason for going further than second-order observations.[5] His point is that a third-order observation (i.e. an observation of an observation of an observation) is structurally similar to a second-order observation in that it, too, observes observation. So moving to the level of third or fourth-order observations offers nothing fundamentally new that is not already accomplished through second-order observations.

## OPERATIVE EPISTEMOLOGY

The assertion that every observation is made by observing systems leads Luhmann to reflect on the relation between observation and reality, and this kind of reflection is unfolded in his epistemological programme. Luhmann's epistemology is founded on input from both the autopoietic turn and the difference-theoretical turn which the Spencer-Brownian influence signifies. Significantly, Luhmann thus states that '[o]ne can answer the question "How is knowledge possible?" with "By the introduction of a distinction" ' (2002d: 130). This Spencer-Brownian framing merely gives rise to a new question, however, for '[b]y means of what distinction is the problem of knowledge articulated?' (2002d: 130). To answer that question Luhmann makes recourse to the system/ environment distinction. This means that when Luhmann examines how we obtain knowledge about the social world, he basically argues that knowledge is possible only through distinctions made by systems that separate themselves from their environment.

To understand the role of the system/environment distinction for Luhmann's conception of knowledge, it might be useful to say a few words on the broader backdrop to Luhmann's epistemological reflections which are inspired by the so-called radical constructivism, advanced by scholars such as Ernst von Glasersfeld and Heinz von Foerster. This constructivist programme should not be conflated with the kind of constructivism which, for example, Peter Berger and Thomas Luckmann have proposed. In their analysis of *The Social Construction of Reality*, the notion of constructivism is used to characterise the dialectical processes by which society appears as an objective reality, but is in fact created by humans (Berger and Luckmann 1966). Institutions play a central role in

Berger and Luckmann's analysis, as these are believed to contribute to socialisation and hence to the continuous reproduction of the social reality. Compared to this sociological conception of constructivism, the radical constructivism of von Glasersfeld and von Foerster operates on a different level. Rather than making claims about the extent to which the reality is a historically-institutionally mediated construction, the radical constructivism is interested in the more fundamental (non-social and rather neurological) conditions of possibility of cognition and knowledge.

The main idea of the radical constructivist programme consists in what appears at first sight to be a rather innocent move: the replacement of one phrase ('in spite of') with another ('because'). Whereas idealist epistemology is concerned with the problem of how knowledge is possible *in spite of* its independent access to the reality, this constructivism takes as its starting point that knowledge is only possible *because* it has no access to the outside reality (Luhmann 1988c: 8–9). Luhmann celebrates this move as a 'relieving radicalisation' of epistemological thought and conceives of it as a way to escape the idea that knowledge is ultimately a question about subject/object relations (1988c: 9). As in his more general considerations on systems theory, Luhmann argues for replacing this conceptual pair with that of system/environment. This not only has the advantage of freeing epistemology from the subject-theoretical tradition, Luhmann claims. The system/environment distinction also proposes a theory-internal correlation to the move from 'in spite of' to 'because'. Thus, as demonstrated in Chapter 2, it is the strict separation of system and environment that allows the system to emerge as an autopoietic entity. The corresponding operational closure, i.e. the ongoing processing of the system, is possible not in spite of its separation from its environment, but because of it. Precisely the same is at stake when it comes to the system's ability to produce knowledge. Knowledge is only possible because the system has no direct access to its environment. An example might illustrate the point. If you lie in bed and press your face down in the pillow, you cannot see the pillow. You need to establish a distance to it in order to be able to observe it. Similarly, a system needs the distance, the boundary, to its environment in order to be able to observe it.

The assertion that no system has direct access to the reality – more precisely, that the system always only has access to the reality through the distinctions it observes with – has two implications. First, it points to Luhmann's emphasis on the operational side of knowledge. Knowledge is only possible through distinctions, i.e. through operations carried out by systems. For this reason he also speaks of his epistemological programme as an 'operative epistemology' (1988c: 21). Second, the above assertion implies that Luhmann's epistemological programme contains no underlying idea of correspondence. Distinctions and hence knowledge are purely internal constructs, and no correlation to the environment can be assumed (2002d: 134–5). In this sense, the reality remains unknown, as the title of one of Luhmann's articles has it (2002d). But as Luhmann repeatedly stresses, this does not amount to saying that there is no reality out there. 'There is an external world – which results from the fact that cognition, as a self-referential operation, can be carried out at all – but we have no direct contact with it' (2002d: 129). So Luhmann's constructivism does not deny the reality, but simply argues that the reality will always only appear to us through the constructions that observers make. This is also where Luhmann's constructivist programme differs from both idealist and realist positions. Contrary to realism, which claims that the reality exists independently of any observer, and to idealism, which asserts that reality is merely something that appears in the mind, Luhmann contends that there is a reality, but that we have no direct access to it. Reality appears through the constructions that observers make. And these constructions are no less real than the 'reality'.

In the same vein, just as no observer has direct access to the reality, so no-one has access to the one and single Truth. This follows directly from the constructivist framework which dissolves the One Truth into a plurality of truths where various observes can claim to possess the truth – each constructed according to the distinctions applied by the particular observer. This does not reduce Luhmann's epistemological programme to a mere relativism where anything goes and where one claim is just as good as any other. Here as elsewhere in his work it is crucial to distinguish between *arbitrary* selections and *contingent* ones. An observation is arbitrary insofar as it is entirely random. Rolling the dice or flipping a coin lead to arbitrary results. But such arbitrariness usually does not apply to knowledge or more generally to the observations of social systems. Social systems make contingent selections, i.e. selections which are neither necessary nor impossible (1998c: 45). But the fact that the selection could have been different does not entail that all other selections were equally likely (as when rolling the dice). Being a sociologist Luhmann is obviously aware that society is characterised by certain social structures which evolve and become more or less stabilised, thereby limiting the possible or at least generally acceptable modes of observation. This applies to knowledge as well. There are always certain social structures that limit the range of possible selections, meaning that even if various observers produce different truths, these truths are not completely random – and therefore also not a sign of relativism.

## ON THE SEARCH FOR PARADOXES

Luhmann (1993c; 1995f) believes that observation constitutes a paradoxical phenomenon since it is refers to the unity of a difference (between distinction and indication). Consequently, the attempt to base his sociological theory on the notion of observation endows it with a paradoxical foundation. This does not evoke concern for Luhmann. Quite the contrary, the third phase of his work is characterised by a veritable search for paradoxes. Whether in the legal field, in art, politics or science, Luhmann constantly traces paradoxes (e.g. 1988e; 2000b: Ch. 9). And he even argues that modern society's functional differentiation gives way to a recurrent stream of paradoxes, as various function systems observe the same phenomena differently (Luhmann 1995f).

It is important to note that Luhmann is not interested in paradoxes from a logical point of view. He distinguishes sharply between a logical and a social approach to paradoxes. While a paradox may appear to the logician as something that brings everything to a standstill, it usually does not pose a great problem in a social context. 'No system is destroyed by logic', Luhmann states, referring to social systems (1989a: 60). For example, everyday experience shows that social systems are not impeded by the fact that they are confronted with paradoxes, that people contradict themselves, etc. In line with this Luhmann's interest in paradoxes is followed by an interest in how they are *de-paradoxified* in practice, as he calls it (1995f: 52). Spencer-Brown's treatise demonstrates how the temporal dimension can be employed to de-paradoxify a paradox by sequencing the operations. But the two other meaning dimensions may also be utilised for this purpose. Thus, argues Luhmann (1999a: 18–20), paradoxes may equally be de-paradoxified or unfolded by introducing a new asymmetry, i.e. by drawing a new distinction (fact dimension); or by observing the observer who is confronted with the paradox (social dimension). In each case, something is done to avoid that the paradox produces a standstill.

On this basis, Luhmann in effect develops a distinctive sociological research programme which traces the paradoxes and de-paradoxifications that social systems face and develop. Alluding to the Gorgon sisters of Greek mythology he characterises this search for paradoxes as 'Sthenography' (referring to Stheno), whereas the search for de-paradoxification is called 'Euryalistic' (after Euryale) (Luhmann 1990j: 120, 124; see also 2002d: 142–3). It might be critically argued that at times Luhmann seems so obsessed with this research programme that his definition of paradoxes becomes rather loose. Elena Esposito has argued that two conditions must be met before it is warranted to speak of a paradox: a paradox is constituted by self-reference and indeterminacy (Esposito 1991: 35–8). The Liar paradox meets these requirements; it is characterised by self-reference ('this sentence …') and by indeterminacy (when true, then false, and vice versa). However, when Luhmann contends that functional differentiation implies a fundamental societal paradox, because society is described differently by the various function systems, then this seems in fact to amount to a contradiction rather than a paradox.

## TOWARD A NEW FOUNDATION: STARTING FROM DIFFERENCE

As I have tried to show in this chapter, Luhmann's enthusiasm for Spencer-Brown's work and the sociological implications he could draw from it meant that Luhmann's systems theory entered a new phase in the late 1980s. This third phase of the oeuvre is characterised by a preoc-cupation with notions such as distinction, form, re-entry, observation, second-order observation, paradox and de-paradoxification. Although these notions carry different meanings and implications, they all start from the concept of difference or distinction. Whereas the second phase of his work was known as the 'autopoietic turn', the third phase might therefore appropriately be called the 'difference-theoretical turn'.

While references to *Laws of Form* do pop up in some of Luhmann's writings from the early 1980s (e.g. Luhmann 1981a; 1995g), the turn to Spencer-Brown and difference theory was not fully heralded before 1988, where Luhmann published a paper entitled 'Frauen, Männer und George Spencer Brown' ['Women, Men and George Spencer Brown'] (Luhmann 1988d; Baecker 1999a: 201, n. 1). This paper presented a very ironically-critical analysis of feminist social theory, based on Spencer-Brown's distinction theory. For present purposes the content of this anal-ysis is not important. I am more interested in *why* Luhmann turned to Spencer-Brown.

This question is all the more pertinent because Luhmann actually points to forerunners within the sociological landscape who, he believes, had argued for founding social theory on an idea of difference. Most notably, Luhmann emphasises Gabriel Tarde, a contemporary of Durkheim, as the first sociologist who started from difference rather than unity. Tarde's sociology is based on the notion of imitation; one person imitates another person and this constitutes the social bond, Tarde argues (see Tarde 1962). According to Luhmann, this notion of imitation is sociologically significant because it always presupposes a difference between the one who imitates and the one who is imitated (Luhmann 1997a: 603, n. 18; 2002a: 68–9; 2006: 39–40).[6] Luhmann also refers to René Girard's (1977) work on mimesis as well as Gregory Bateson's work on information, defined as 'a difference which makes a difference' (2000: 315), as congenial positions in the sense that they too start from difference (Luhmann 2002a: 69; 2006: 40). It is nevertheless Spencer-Brown who receives Luhmann's greatest attention. Why can that be? And how come the obsession with Spencer-Brownian terms explodes in the late 1980s, while they only occupy a rather marginal role in publications from the early 1980s.

To answer these questions it might be useful to consider the strategic functions that Spencer-Brown's treatise seemed to serve for Luhmann. Specifically, I would argue, Spencer-Brown's work enabled Luhmann to relate his systems theory to the deconstructivist – and more generally poststructuralist – movement that gained much popularity in the 1980s and 1990s. Luhmann could simply use the notions of observation, paradox, re-entry, etc. to formulate his sociological counterpart and correction to Jacques Derrida's programme. This found its most obvious expression in articles such as 'Deconstruction as Second-Order Observing' (Luhmann 1993b). Here as elsewhere Luhmann shows great respect for Derrida. In Luhmann's view, one of Derrida's chief accomplishments is that '[d]econstruction draws attention to the fact that differences are only distinctions and change their use value when we use them at different times and in different contexts' (1993b: 764). For example, Luhmann added, the 'difference between heterosexuals and homosexuals is not always the same'; in the army this distinction has certain meanings and effects; in a religious context it has other meanings and effects (1993b: 764). While Luhmann subscribed to this context-specific understanding of distinctions, he believed that deconstruction failed to account for the observer drawing the distinctions and he therefore stressed the need 'to replace *deconstruction* with *second-order observing*' (1993b: 776, italics in original). In effect Luhmann argued that deconstruction should be celebrated for a number of achievements but that it did not take the full step and therefore required a sociological superstructure that systems theory and the turn to second-order observation could supply.[7]

At the same time, it seems fair to contend that Spencer-Brown served a mystifying function as well. *Laws of Form* thus allowed Luhmann to play on the almost cultist endorsement of the treatise that had emerged within cybernetic circles (Knodt 1995: 492, n. 12). So even if the attempt to relate systems theory to deconstruction aimed in part to capitalise on the popularity that Derrida's work enjoyed, it seems that Luhmann was happy to endow his sociological theory with a vocabulary that was arguably even more alienating to most sociologists than the previous autopoietic framing had been. As an illustration of this, he once introduced a lecture, which through its title, 'Observing Re-entries', pointed to Spencer-Brownian notions, by saying to the audience that 'I enjoy the idea that the title of my lecture will not be understandable to you' (Luhmann 1993c: 485).

Leaving these strategic speculations aside, it is important to stress that the difference-theoretical turn did not entirely revolutionise Luhmann's theoretical focus. Much of the vocabulary was new, but several earlier theoretical interests and observations were pertained. For example, Luhmann maintained his diagnosis of modern society as functionally differentiated, just as he continued describing social systems in terms of autopoiesis, operational closure and structural couplings. Still, the difference-theoretical turn did instigate a new agenda both with respect to Luhmann's previous scholarly emphases and in terms of his strategic framing or 'branding' of the theory where the main play-mates were no longer Habermas and action theory, but rather Derrida.

Moreover, a number of previous key terms were now reinterpreted in light of the new vocabulary. I will give just a few examples of this. Most notably, perhaps, the notion of systems was defined as nothing but a specific kind of difference: 'a system *is* the difference between system and environment' (Luhmann 2006: 38, italics in original; see also 1999b: 49). The unity of the system is its difference. Consequently, it is obvious that Luhmann did not found his theory on a basic identity, but rather on difference. For Luhmann, difference is at the heart of the social reality. Had it not been clear before, this radical difference-theoretical conception of systems separated Luhmann's theory completely from any Parsonian legacy. Equally significantly, communi-cation, the defining feature of social systems, was redefined in observa-tion terms. Thus, argues Luhmann in *Die Gesellschaft der Gesellschaft*, communication is not merely a threefold selection of information, utterance and understanding; communication is the *observation* of the *difference* between information and utterance (1997a: 72). Similarly, the notion of meaning was given a Spencer-Brownian twist, namely as the form of distinction of actuality and potentiality (Luhmann 1990a: 108–10; 2002c: 121).

# 4

# The functional differentiation of modern society

## LUHMANN'S TWO APPROACHES TO DIFFERENTIATION

The previous chapters have established the conceptual foundation and main assumptions of Luhmann's systems theory. This has been rather abstract and deliberately so since Luhmann's explicit aim is to develop a grand social theory that can account for all social phenomena. It is now time to move to his more specific analyses of modern society. The central claim underlying these analyses is that modern society is characterised by a particular kind of differentiation: it is differentiated into a series of operationally autonomous subsystems that fulfil each their function for society.

Studying modernity and modern society on basis of an idea of differentiation is not new. As Luhmann states, '[e]ver since there has been sociological theory it has been concerned with social differentiation' (1990c: 409). In Marx' work this was formulated as an interest in the differentiation between the economic base and the political-ideological superstructure of society. Durkheim argued that modern society was characterised by an elaborated division of labour which produced a new form of organic solidarity (Durkheim 1964). Simmel examined modern society's increasing differentiation and its consequences for individuality

(Simmel 1989). Weber observed a differentiation and rationalisation of distinct 'value spheres' (the economy, religion, the erotic, politics, aesthetics and intellectualism), each endowed with its own particular logic (Weber 1920: 536 ff.). Parsons saw modern society as differentiated into four main subsystems each fulfilling their central function: the economy (the function of adaptation), the polity/political subsystem (specialising in goal attainment), the societal community (providing integration) and the so-called fiduciary system (dedicated to latent pattern maintenance) (Parsons and Smelser 1956). It is not only these famous sociological classics that discuss differentiation as a key societal phenomenon. More recent sociologists also focus on societal differentiation (e.g. Alexander and Colomy 1990). For example, the sociology of Pierre Bourdieu might be seen as presenting a contemporary attempt to rethink societal differentiation along a new understanding of fields and forms of capital.

Luhmann stands on the shoulders of this sociological tradition, which places the question of differentiation centrally for the understanding of modern society, but he offers his own distinctive conception of differentiation, which differs in many respects from that of other sociologists. In fact, Luhmann might be said to propose two general approaches to differentiation. On a general level of systems modality, he argues that social systems can be divided into three main types, namely interactions, organisations and societies (see Figure 2.1).[1] While this differentiation is rather independent of the classic sociological discussions, he also contributes more directly to debates on how modern society is differentiated. The two levels (social systems and society) are related, however, and will be discussed in turn below. I will begin with the differentiation between interactions, organisations and societies and will then proceed with the theme of societal differentiation, which will constitute the main bulk of this chapter. This latter discussion will address the central elements in Luhmann's theory of modern society and its functional differentiation. This includes a view to how function systems are organised as well as a discussion of the evolutionary aspects of the functional differentiation (codes, programmes, symbolically generalised media of communication, etc.).

## INTERACTION, ORGANISATION, SOCIETY

To begin with, Luhmann's differentiation of social systems into interactions, organisations and societies approximates a distinction between micro, meso, and macro.[2] *Interaction systems* are defined by co-presence and reflexive perception and refer basically to the kind of face-to-face communication that Erving Goffman has analysed.[3] Importantly, interaction systems require *both* co-presence *and* reflexive perception. If one of these conditions is not met, there is no interaction system. So, for example, the mere fact that two or more people are physically present in the same room at the same time does not produce interaction. The interaction system only emerges when this co-presence is combined with reflexive perception, which refers to a situation where communication partners not merely perceive other co-present people, but perceive their perceptions. Sitting in a train, for instance, an interaction system emerges between the other passengers and me when I begin to regulate my behaviour according to how I think the others perceive me. I perceive that the other passengers perceive me and vice versa, and this organises the communication (which may well be non-verbal).

Luhmann has written relatively little on interaction systems (most significantly, 1975b; 1975a).[4] One might speculate that this has two primary reasons. First, his notion of interaction is modelled so closely around Goffman's work that Luhmann might have thought that he could add nothing substantially new to this topic. Second, Luhmann's interest in interaction systems is limited because of the scarce amount of complexity they can process. Since interaction systems rely on co-presence, they face social, temporal, but also factual limitations: there are limits to the number of people who can be part of an interaction system; there are limits to how long people can be physically co-present (and therefore how long the interaction system can be maintained); just as there are limits to the number of topics that can be meaningfully discussed within one interaction system (no specialisation is possible within an interaction system). So although one can hardly think of a society which does not contain a large number of interaction systems, highly complex modern societies must find ways of handling complexity that do not rely on face-to-face interactions. This is one of the reasons for Luhmann's continuous interest in organisations, the second general category of social systems he analyses.

Contrary to interaction systems, *organisations* are able to deal with problems and communications that extend far beyond the realm of co-present people. They can also acquire more stabilised structures, as they can exist for centuries (think of religious organisations). According to Luhmann, organisations are characterised by two central features: they have rules for *membership* and operate by making *decisions* (Luhmann 2000d). Of course, these decisions are only valid to the members of the organisation. People who are not members of, say, a fan club need not adhere to its decisions. The membership rules work in effect as a means of social exclusion. Not all can be members of the organisation; if it included everybody, there would be nothing to distinguish it from society as such. This exclusiveness in terms of membership is compensated, as it were, by factual inclusiveness. An organisation can in principle devote itself to any topic. To illustrate, the group of wine enthusiasts becomes an organisation when it establishes criteria for membership. For example, it may decide only to allow members who are dedicated to French rather than Italian, Spanish, etc. winemakers. Over the years, however, the wine organisation might gradually change. It might be that the members' lobbying efforts for financial support to French winemakers eventually transforms the organisation into a political party, which ultimately needs to take a stance on all sorts of political issues (healthcare, crime rates, bank regulation, social exclusion, etc.) which did not form part of its initial concerns.

As indicated, one of the great advantages of organisations relates to their temporal horizons which go far beyond that of interaction systems. An organisation, whether a political party, a corporation, a fan club, etc., can continue to exist even if its members are replaced. This allows for organisational specialisation and hence for handling great amounts of complexity. For this reason Luhmann argues that formal organisations are becoming increasingly important in modern society. This has to do with another exceptional feature of organisations, namely their capacity to connect to and bridge over functionally differentiated systems (economy, politics, art, law, etc.). For example, a corporation will usually have to be able to communicate economically (products or services are sold, taxes and wages must be paid), legally (adhere to the regulation that applies to its field of operation), politically (interpreting what might be politically opportune in the future), etc. That is, organisations are not necessarily bound to only one function system, although some of course might be primarily economic (a company), political (a party organisation), scientific (a university), etc.[5] While this cross-functional ability might seem trivial, it is not, Luhmann claims. To understand this it is important to dive into the third basic kind of social system that Luhmann analyses: *society*.

Society is the sum of all communication, according to Luhmann. But as a sociologist he obviously has much more to say about society than this. As mentioned in Chapter 2, his main approach to discussing society revolves around society's primary mode of differentiation. Contrary to the segmentary and stratificatory modes of differentiation that characterised pre-modern societies, Luhmann argues that the key defining trait of modern society is its functional differentiation.

## FUNCTIONAL DIFFERENTIATION: ONE FUNCTION, ONE SYSTEM

What does Luhmann understand by functional differentiation? Very basically, the notion refers to the development by which society becomes differentiated into a number of operationally autonomous societal subsystems each of which fulfils a specific function in and for society. This functional component sets function systems apart from other social systems, such as organisations and interactions. Luhmann contends that it is possible to identify function systems of law, economy, politics, art, education, science, religion and the mass media. These are the main function systems that Luhmann analyses. It is an empirical question, however, how many function systems exist, so other function systems might be identified, even if Luhmann did not do so himself.[6]

Function systems have earned their name because they are said by Luhmann to fulfil a specific societal function. This function defines their reference to society as such. However, the reference to society is only one of three system references for function systems. According to Luhmann, each function system can:

> gear its selective operations toward three distinct system refer-
> ences: (1) toward the *system of society* in terms of its *function*; (2)
> toward *other subsystems* within society's internal environment in
> terms of *input and output performances*; and (3) toward *itself* in terms
> of *self-reflection*.

> (1982c: 238, italics in original)

So the function describes the particular contribution the function system offers to society; the performance refers to the contributions that function systems offer to one another; and the reflection to the system's observations of itself, typically in the form of self-descriptions. In the following, I am mainly interested in the first two system references.

According to Luhmann, the function of the political system is to make collectively binding decisions for society, whereas the function of the legal system is to maintain society's generalised normative expectations (to be explained in more detail below). The crucial point is that the function which is fulfilled by each function system is fulfilled by this system only and cannot be fulfilled by other systems. In this sense each function system is unique and cannot be substituted. Luhmann also speaks of a 'renouncement of redundancy' (1997a: 761) to account for this, which is another way of saying that the function fulfilled by one function system is fulfilled by this system alone. This makes possible great internal specialisation. The function monopoly, as it were, of each function system allows the system to develop continuously so as to handle increasing amounts of complexity. At the same time, the function monopoly entails an enormous latent risk, as the potential collapse of a function system cannot be remedied by other function systems. I will discuss the performances of function systems below when addressing the relations between function systems. First, however, I wish to examine another unique feature of function systems, namely their so-called binary codes.

## BINARY CODES

Luhmann argues that every function system is organised around its particular binary code, which the system uses to see and interpret the world. Importantly, the binary codes are, as the name suggests, strictly binary. They have only two values and any other values are excluded. For example, the system of science is characterised by the code true/false, meaning that every observation the system makes is filtered through this code. The system can only approach the world through this code, and everything that cannot be fitted into it is deemed irrelevant by the system. This touches upon an important aspect of functional differentiation: that each function system produces an 'intense *sensibility to specific questions*' (namely those that fall within its specialised focus) and at the same time a great '*indifference towards everything else*', including the operational logics of other systems (Luhmann 1990d: 31, italics in original). So not only are function systems, like all other social systems, operationally closed; they are closed around their binary codes which prevents them from adopting the perspectives of other systems. Or in a more positive formulation, the binary code frees the function system of the burden of having to take into account what other systems consider important.

For example, the economic function system's basic concern is with payments, and its binary code is payment/non-payment. When you are in a shop the only thing that matters to the economic system is whether or not you can pay for the goods. Whether you are member of a certain political party, subscribes to a particular religious faith or have success in love does not matter to the economic system. Similarly, the system of science is indifferent to economic fortune, in the sense that whether or not you are wealthy has no bearing on the assessment of your scientific work. Here the only question that matters is whether you are on the side of true or false. So in a functionally differentiated society, scientific success cannot be bought, it does not follow from influential political friends, nor does it rely on one's marital status. Science's criteria for assessing scientific observations are wholly scientific; just as the economy's criteria for assessing economic observations are completely economic, etc.[7]

Luhmann's assertion that the differentiation of codes and function systems produces an indifference to what cannot be fitted into the code's two values also contains another important aspect. Thus, he claims, the various binary codes are independent in the sense that they cannot be equated with a moral coding of good and bad.[8] For example, the political system's code government/opposition cannot meaningfully be reduced to moral categories. Similarly, there is no inherently moral division in the scientific system's code, true/false. It is not morally better, for instance, to be on the side of truth rather than falseness. Luhmann draws the full implications of this and argues that '[t]he function systems are coded at the *level of a higher amorality*' (1987b: 25, italics added; see also 1990b: 51; 1994c; 1997a: 751). Consequently, and this is the more implicit theoretical agenda that seems to be at stake here, sociological theories that revolve around moral evaluations of society and its function systems do not hit the target. They fail to see the fundamentally amoral (not necessarily *im*moral) constitution of modern society.

## CODE CLASHES AND PROGRAMMES

Binary codes are defining features of function systems. Function systems organise their observations and operations around them. In most situations this proceeds smoothly. The economic system pursues its operations according to the payment/non-payment code, and it is easy to detect that this is the case, Luhmann believes. The same applies to the political system, the legal system, etc. Yet while it is usually easy to say which system reference is at stake in a given situation (are we dealing with a payment, a legal decision, a scientific observation, etc.?), at times this cannot easily be discerned. Let me give a few examples. If a researcher is studying a topic in which he or she has clear economic interests, can we be sure that the research is independent and not affected by economic considerations? Can we be sure, in other words, that the scientific findings have not been perverted so as to reflect what is most economically advantageous to the researcher? Here confusion arises as to which binary code is employed, and concern arises because the strict separation between function systems might be in danger. Likewise, if a politician attempts to change existing legal regulation which affects him or her negatively, the separation between the binary codes of the political and legal systems threatens to dissolve, once again giving rise to concern and confusion. As a final illustration, discussions of set matches in sport are ultimately an example of the binary codes of sport (winning/losing) and economy being confused. Here it becomes impossible to say which system is really at work: is the result of a soccer match a consequence of fair competition or a function of economic interests? The analytical point is that Luhmann's theory of functional differentiation offers a way to study and understand these and similar code clashes. ('Code clashes' is not a Luhmann term, though.) Each of these cases produces concern and confusion, precisely because it questions the functional differentiation that we take for granted.

Somewhat related to code clashes are situations where function systems share an operation, i.e. where the same occurrence, the same communication, is part of two systems simultaneously. Luhmann uses the term 'operative couplings' to describe this (2004: 381). For example, to pay a fine is at once a legal operation (an implementation of a punishment) and an economic communication (a transaction). Examples of operative couplings apparently conflict with Luhmann's insistence that every system, including function systems, is characterised by one type of operation only, for this assertion implies that every operation can be part of only one system. Yet, states Luhmann, operative couplings do not really challenge the one system–one operation dogma. The reason is that operative couplings only exist in the instantaneous moment of the operation. The connecting operations will go in different directions in the systems that are operationally coupled. For example, '[t]he economic aspect of a payment, which relates to the reuse of money, is quite different from the legal aspect, which relates to the change in the legal situation induced by the payment' (Luhmann 2004: 381).

It follows from this that operative couplings need not question the separation of function systems; they might be coupled in the very event of the operation but from then on they follow their own paths, without creating confusion and concern. But what, then, distinguishes a code clash from an operative coupling? When is the intermingling of systems a problem, and when not? Luhmann gives no decisive answer to this. Ultimately, it is an empirical question whether or not an operative coupling is observed as a code clash. It can be stated, though, that code clashes occur whenever suspicion emerges that the operations of one system is regulated, not according to the system's own criteria but rather according to the criteria of other systems. For example, the researcher presents his or her findings *as if* there were scientific, but fellow scientists observe the findings as guided by personal economic interests. So code clashes emerge when observers observe an overlap of binary codes, and this might be triggered when perceiving momentary operative couplings.

The reference to the criteria for regulating the use of binary codes leads to a broader discussion, which is not per se related to problems of code clashes and operative couplings. It has been stressed that function systems operate on basis of their binary codes. However, the binary codes do not themselves suggest how they be applied. For example, the scientific system's code true/false does not itself make clear when the system can describe a finding as true or false. In order to find ways of regulating the use of the code, systems develop what Luhmann calls *programmes*, which designate 'given conditions for the suitability of the selection of operations' (1989a: 45; see also 1995g: 317). That is, programmes define the conditions for attributing the code's values correctly. Every function system develops its own specific programmes. The system of science, for instance, develops theories and methods which the system then applies for assessing whether a particular finding is true or not: did the research follow recognised theories and methods, or were the findings based on completely arbitrary procedures? In the latter case, it would not be possible to consider the finding scientifically true. Similarly, in the economic system, prices function as programmes that enable the system to decide whether a payment is correct or not.

The combination of codes and programmes endows function systems with a simultaneous stability and flexibility, closure and openness. The binary codes are not open for change. The legal system cannot suddenly invent a new code, such as slow/fast, to replace legal/illegal. This unchangeability of codes ensures stability and is a means through which the function system enacts its operational closure. The legal system is and remains interested solely in the code of legal/illegal, and it employs this code to organise its selections. Programmes, by contrast, can be modified and even replaced with new programmes. For example, in the scientific system the programmes (theories and methods) undergo continual change. New theories are developed which replace old ones, and the same applies to methods. It is even possible that new types of scientific programmes could emerge alongside theories and methods. For example, Niels Åkerstrøm Andersen argues for replacing the focus on methods with an attentiveness to what he calls 'analytical strategies' (Andersen 2003). Such a change in focus in effect introduces a new programme for how science considers a given finding true or false. This means that the criteria which the system uses to select either true or false are in flux. What is considered accepted theories and methods in one historical context can look rather different in another context.

The more general point is that all the inflexibility which the code embodies is compensated for by a high degree of flexibility on the level of programmes. This flexibility also endows the system with openness.

The programmes provide a way for the function systems to adapt to a changing environment. For example, the fall of the Berlin Wall in 1989 and the subsequent dissolution of the Soviet Union induced a new theoretical apparatus to understand global politics, in particular East–West relations. Much pre-1989 theorising on this topic was all of a sudden obsolete. The scientific system was able to adapt to this new situation. While the system's code remained the same, the theories that were used as programmes to chose true or false could change and thereby ensure that the system developed along the historic dynamics.

However, in one particular sense the programmes are just as inflexible as the binary codes. Thus, claims Luhmann (1989a: 46–7), every programme is code specific; it provides criteria for assessing which of the two sides of a specific binary code should be applied in a given context. This means that the programmes that are employed to direct the use of one code cannot be employed to direct the use of another code. Theories and methods of the scientific system cannot help the political system to determine when which of its binary code's two sides, government/opposition, applies.

## SYMBOLICALLY GENERALISED MEDIA OF COMMUNICATION

Functional differentiation did not evolve out of the blue. In his examination of the evolutionary backdrop to this mode of differentiation, Luhmann pays primary attention to what he calls *symbolically generalised media of communication*. These media themselves have a specific historical background, as they serve to handle the fundamental problem of social order that has ridden social thinkers from Thomas Hobbes onward: How, in a state of nature, can order arise when A and B are confronted with one another and when the other part's action is unpredictable? What mechanism can ensure that some order emerges in such an indeterminate state? Hobbes suggested a sovereign, the Leviathan, to solve the problem. By enforcing a strong political regime, where disobedience is strongly punished, the sovereign is able to create and maintain a social order. Luhmann's solution takes a very different form. He approaches the problem of social order by framing it as a question of the *double contingency* of selections. The notion of double contingency is inherited from Parsons. In Luhmann's adaptation, it refers to the problem of how ego's selections 'will be accepted by alter as premise of his own selections' (1976: 511). The question then is, how can it be made likely that some coordination takes place between ego's and alter's selections? How, in other words, is it made possible that 'essentially improbable communications' between ego and alter will nevertheless be successful (Luhmann 1998a: 18)?

Such questions might seem speculative, for why should communication be improbable? Why speak of improbability when a mass-mediated everyday life suggests the very opposite, namely a veritable overload of communication? To understand this, it is necessary to recognise how deep Luhmann seeks to dig in his investigation. His ambition is to answer the most fundamental question of sociology, namely how communication, and hence society, is possible. To do so he brings together his focus on communication and his conceptualisation of double contingency as a matter of selections. More specifically, he takes as his starting point 'a contra-phenomenological effort, viewing communication not as a phenomenon but as a problem' (Luhmann 1990l: 87). Following this perspective, it is possible to identify three key obstacles to communication, states Luhmann. 'At the zero point of evolution, it is, first of all, improbable that ego *understands* what alter means – given that their bodies and minds are separate and individual' (Luhmann 1995g: 158, italics in original). The second problem is spatio-temporal. 'It is improbable that a communication should reach more persons than are present in a given situation' (1990l: 88). This problem intensifies in a modern complex society which cannot rely on face-to-face communication. How, in such a society, is it made probable that people living in different parts of the world can and will communicate? Finally, the third problem is what Luhmann refers to as the 'improbability of success':

> Even if a communication is understood, there can be no assurance of its being accepted. By "success" I mean that the recipient of the communication accepts the selective content of the communication (the information) as a premise of his own behavior.
>
> (1990l: 88)

This improbability refers to whether communication has any effects. Does communication lead the addressee to change his or her behaviour, or is the information merely understood but then ignored or rejected? According to Luhmann, it is improbable that communication does in fact change the behaviour of the addressee.

The three improbabilities are all obstacles to creating a social order. So for communication and social order to be made probable devices must be developed that increase the likelihood that communication will take place and, consequently, that social systems emerge. Importantly, such devices also respond to the problem of double contingency which is weaved into the improbability issue, especially the improbability of success. Luhmann argues that throughout history various media have evolved which work as such devices. In this context, media should not be conflated with mass media. Luhmann has an entirely different understanding in mind. For him, media refer to mechanisms 'involved in transforming improbable into probable communication' (1990l: 89).

Specifically, he distinguishes between three key media. One is *language* which gives a sense of common understanding among communication partners, thereby increasing the probability of communication (and addressing especially the first of the above-mentioned improbabilities). Based on the existence of language, *media of dissemination* have evolved, including writing, printing, radio, television, and more recently the internet (1995g: 161). As the name suggests, these media offer a solution to the spatio-temporal improbability of communication. In spite of their achievements, however, Luhmann insists that neither language nor dissemination media are able to handle the improbability of success. That is, neither of these media contains motivations that increase the probability that the recipient of communication accepts the information as a premise for his or her behaviour. This motivation is offered only by so-called *symbolically generalised media of communication*:

> We would like to call "symbolically generalized" the media that use generalizations to symbolize the nexus between selection and motivation, that is, represent it as a unity. Important examples are: truth, love, property/money, power/law; and also, in rudimentary form, religious belief, art, and, today, standardized "basic values." In all these cases this – in a very different way and for very different interactive constellations – is a matter of conditioning the selection of communication so that it also works as a means of motivation, that is, so that it can adequately secure acceptance of the proposed selection.
>
> (1995g: 161)

More specifically, the *symbolically generalised* nature of these media refers to the fact that they can be used in very different contexts; they do not specify the content to which they are applied (Luhmann 1976: 520). For example, money is a general medium that can be used all over the world, and money itself does not specify when and in what situations it could serve to facilitate communication.

It is crucial to note that, for Luhmann, symbolically generalised media of communication are analysed *functionally*, namely as a solution to the problem of double contingency: they offer each their (functionally equivalent) way of making probable that communication is successful and that ego's selections will be accepted by alter as premise for his or her own selections. Consequently, the symbolically generalised media of communication provide a solution to the fundamental sociological problem of how social order is possible.

In order to understand *how* more specifically each of the symbolically generalised media of communication fulfil this function, as well as how they differ from one another in their functionally equivalent contributions, Luhmann distinguishes not only between the selections of ego and alter, but also between selections that relate to either experience or action. In a sense, this generates a doubling of the problem of double contingency. Luhmann thus claims that symbolically generalised media of communication are differentiated according to how they coordinate the selections of ego's experience and action with alter's experience and action. This opens for four distinct constellations:

(1) The experience of alter may be accepted as vicarious experience of ego (Ae ➜ Ee). (2) The experience of alter may be accepted by ego in the form of a corresponding action (Ae ➜ Ea). (3) The action of alter may select an experience of ego and be accepted as such (Aa ➜ Ee). (4) The action of alter may be accepted as action of ego (Aa ➜ Ea).

(1976: 515)

This is certainly very abstract. Luhmann's (more comprehensible) point is that, historically, a series of symbolically generalised media of communication have emerged which offer each their way of coping with one of the alter–ego constellations. Thus, the medium of *truth* makes alter's experience a premise for ego's experience. By making recourse to scientific truths, it is likely that alter's experience is accepted by ego as the foundation for his or her experience. This is what happens in the case of learning, states Luhmann: 'Learning from others, he [ego, CB] accepts on notice experiences as results of selection processes without taking the pain, or the time, or even without being able to repeat these processes' (1976: 516). The symbolically generalised medium of truth therefore at once reduces complexity and handles the problem of double contingency; alter can transmit experiences to ego, without ego having to question them, and this is accepted by ego because the transmission takes place in the medium of truth. According to Luhmann, *values* might be seen as another, but weaker, medium that connects alter's experience to ego's experience. Abstract values such as human rights provide a normative framework that binds experiences to one another. Yet due to their abstractness, they only mediate experience; they do not suggest actions (1997a: 340–4).

Similarly, *love* is a medium specialised in handling 'highly personalized' communication (Luhmann 1998a: 20). It does so by linking the experience of the beloved (alter) to the action of the lover (ego). That is, the lover (ego) must confirm through his or her action that he or she loves the beloved (alter) even if the latter is only interested in his or her idiosyncratic experiences (1997a: 345; 1998a: 22–3). *Property* and later *money* work as media that link alter's action to ego's experience. The use of money ensures that alter's action, e.g. the consumption of some scarce goods, does not provoke ego to act, but merely induces ego's experience and acceptance of alter's action. Alter was able to pay for goods, and so ego accepts that alter, and not ego, is now in possession of the goods. According to Luhmann, *art* too connects alter's action with ego's experience: the artist acts and the spectator experiences the art piece, whether in the gallery or at home (1997a: 351; see also 1990n).

Finally, Luhmann argues, *law* and *power* are the media through which alter's action is turned into the premise for ego's action. Taking only power as the example, the referee (alter) gives a soccer player (ego) a yellow card, which curbs the latter's aggressive style. Or more positively, the manager (alter) introduces a new bonus system, which stimulates the employee (ego) to work harder. Luhmann's differentiation of the symbolically generalised media of communication is illustrated in Table 4.1.

It might be critically argued that Luhmann's conception of symbolically differentiated media of communication is far from self-explanatory. Not only may the very difference between action and experience be questioned, a difference which Luhmann admits is 'somewhat artificial' (1979: 119). It also is not obvious why, for example, love is a matter of action on ego's side and not experience (as well), and why power could not concern the experience of ego and not just his or her action. Be that as it may. For present purposes, I do not wish to engage in a critique of Luhmann's theory of symbolically generalised media of communication. I am more interested in the function it serves in his overall theoretical framework. For in addition to providing an answer to the problem of double contingency and the improbability of communication, the theory of symbolically generalised media of communication is tightly connected

*Table 4.1* Symbolically Generalised Media of Communication (adapted from Luhmann, 1997a: 336)

| Alter/Ego | Experience | Action |
|---|---|---|
| Experience | Ae ➔ Ee | Ae ➔ Ea |
|  | Truth/values | Love |
| Action | Aa ➔ Ee | Aa ➔ Ea |
|  | Property/money/art | Power/law |

to the theory of functional differentiation. Luhmann thus argues that these media triggered the differentiation of function systems (1976: 515, 518–9; 1997a: 358). That is, functional differentiation was only possible on the basis of a differentiation of symbolically generalised media of communication.[9] More specifically, Luhmann purports, this development of functional differentiation was prompted when the symbolically generalised media provided a code structure (the binary codes) which the functional differentiation could evolve around (1997a: 359 ff.). So each of the media gave way to a specific binary code (e.g. payment/non-payment for the medium of money), and this constituted the backdrop to the development of independent, autopoietic and operationally closed function systems.[10]

## THE FUNCTION SYSTEMS

Having delineated the fundamental characteristics of function systems, it is now time to give an outline of the various function systems that Luhmann analyses (Luhmann provides an overview of some of these systems in 1989a). Needless to say, the below account cannot go into detail with all the function systems, let alone fully account for just one of them. After all, Luhmann wrote thick books about each of these systems and even devoted more books to a couple of systems, such as law and religion. So very much in line with the mantra of Luhmann's early sociology, quite some complexity must be reduced in the following. I will proceed in two tempi. First, I will look at the political system, the legal system and the economic system, and in each case outline the system's function, binary code, programmes as well as its symbolically generalised medium of communication. The account of these systems will be compressed but still somewhat extensive. I will then turn to the other function systems that Luhmann has studied, namely science, religion, art, the mass media and education. These systems will only be presented extremely briefly, just listing their respective function, code, etc. There is no particular reason for giving more space to the political, legal and economic systems at the expense of the other ones. This selection certainly does not reflect that these three systems are more important than the others for, as I will come back to in Chapter 5, functional differentiation implies that there is no hierarchy among function systems.

### The political system

The function of the political system 'can be characterized as *supplying the capacity to enforce collectively binding decisions*' (1990d: 73, italics in original). Although other systems such as the economy (e.g. during a financial crisis) or religion (e.g. when the Pope addresses his followers) may also, both in principle and in practice, have widespread effects and affect people in many different situations, it is only the political system that can make decisions which are collectively binding and which can be enforced legitimately over the entire population. The political system can make decisions which have to be accepted even if one disagrees with them. In order to enforce these decision (and thereby avoid sheer anarchy), the political system can make recourse, if needed, to physical force. Luhmann therefore agrees with Max Weber that the political system has the monopoly on the legitimate use of physical force (1990d: 74; Weber 1978: 54).

According to Luhmann, there is an intimate connection between the political system and the symbolically generalised medium of power. To be sure, power might be applied in all sorts of situations (the parent exercising power over the child; the teacher over the pupil; the employer over the employee, etc.). As such power is 'distributed diffusely' in society (2000b: 74). There is nevertheless an intense concentration of power in the political system. Power is quite simply 'the quintessence of politics', states Luhmann (2000b: 75). I shall discuss Luhmann's conception of power in more detail in Chapter 6. For now it suffices to note that since power is about regulating (ego's) actions through (alter's) actions, it makes sense to distinguish crudely between the power–holder (alter) and the power–subject (ego).[11] Luhmann argues that this distinction is transformed and fixated in the political system, where it appears as the separation between government (the power–holder) and opposition (the power–subject), designating who is and who is not currently holding political office.

The distinction between government and opposition is the binary code that guides the political system's daily operations. Every political theme can be divided according to this difference. The opposition will typically argue that the government does too little or that it makes the wrong decisions (in foreign policy, on unemployment, for the elderly, in terms of crime prevention, etc., etc.) and that it, the opposition, could do things much better. The government, on its side, will claim the very opposite, namely that the opposition should show greater responsibility and back up the decisions made by the government; that the government is the true guarantor for societal well-being and that the opposition will only bring destabilisation and insecurity should it gain power.

The political system has various procedures and programmes that regulate the use of the government/opposition code. Most importantly, a combination of constitutions and elections provide the conditions for determining who is entitled to hold office for a given time period (Luhmann's confines his analysis to democratic political systems). The government and the opposition have each their political programmes, which articulate their propositions for which collectively binding decisions should be made in the various policy areas. Yet the party which is presently holding political office has the advantage that its programmes will serve as the basis for the political decision-making; or, at least until the next election where the current opposition may obtain its goal and replace the government. The political system will be discussed in more detail in Chapter 6.

## The legal system

Whereas the political system is occupied with collectively binding decisions, the legal system's communications are concerned with expectations. Thus, states Luhmann, the function of law lies in the 'stabilization of normative expectations' (2004: 148). To recall the distinction between normative and cognitive expectations introduced in Chapter 2, normative expectations refer to expectations that are retained even if they are disappointed. According to Luhmann, expectations are essentially about time, and more specifically about the future. So when Luhmann claims that law's function is to stabilise normative expectations this entails a dissociation from classical assertions, put forward for example by Durkheim (1964), that law fulfils an integrating function in society, or that law serves to perform social control (see Luhmann 2004: 143). Rather than focusing on this social dimension of law that Durkheim studies, Luhmann asserts that law's function must be understood with respect to its temporal dimension.

Luhmann's argument runs as follow. Since the future is inherently uncertain, normative expectations are created which serve to link the present and the future – a kind of 'time binding' as Luhmann (2004: 145) calls it. For example, it is well-known that conflicts may arise in the future. In order to handle this problem and to ensure that potential future conflicts neither escalate nor obstruct present communication, normative expectations are formulated in the present which can regulate future conflicts, *should they occur.* The last addition is crucial: normative expectations are essentially counterfactual; they refer to future occurrences which need not take place at all. To summarise this, '[l]aw's relation to time lies […] in the function of norms, that is, in the attempt to anticipate, at least on the level of expectations, a still unknown, genuinely uncertain future' (2004: 147). By establishing what is legal and what is illegal (the binary code of the legal system), the law makes it possible to make expectations about what the future is likely to bring and not to bring, even if this future remains uncertain. For example, by making violence illegal the law allows for the expectation that it is possible to move freely in the street. Should violence nevertheless occur, the legal system can sanction the deed and thereby stabilise the expectation that violence is illegal and will be punished.

The focus on expectations to an unknown future may also be conceptualised on the basis of the problem of double contingency. Just as power works as a medium for the political system, which ensures that alter's action is used as premise for ego's action, so the legal system links alter's action and ego's action through its symbolically generalised medium of law. Law provides a normative framework that permits alter to expect that his or her action will form the premise for ego's action (see Luhmann 1987c: 32 ff.). For example, alter and ego enter a contract with one another about some topic (e.g. a financial transaction). By enforcing contract regulation, the law ensures that the contract is used by ego to guide his or her subsequent action. Should ego violate the contract, alter can refer to the law and thereby enforce the stipulated action. This example points to another crucial aspect of the legal system, according to Luhmann. For although the law might be employed to solve conflicts in society (one of law's performances, see 2004: 168–72), it is also and 'first and foremost a means of creating them' (1995g: 331): due to the existence of law, it is possible to make claims about mistreatment, violence, fraud, etc. and thereby to give communications a legal, conflictual framing.

The legal system organises its communications through the binary code legal/illegal, so everything that law observes is filtered through this code. Law does not consider whether a specific occurrence is artistic, beautiful or academically interesting; it is solely interested in establishing whether it is legal or illegal. In order to guide the use of this code, the legal system employs specific programmes such as legal norms (laws, previous legal decisions, etc.) and courtroom proceedings. These programmes can undergo great changes. This might be illustrated through the historical transformations in criminal law's programmes for how to sanction (see Borch 2005a). In the nineteenth century, much criminal law focused on *offences*. If the legal system determined that an offence (an illegality) had taken place, a punishment was meted out which corresponded to the graveness of the deed. By contrast, especially in the first half of the twentieth century, the focus shifted from the offence to the *offender*: If the legal system determined that a violation of criminal law had taken place, the sanction was measured, not according to how grave the offence was, but rather according to how dangerous the offender was considered to be.

In either case, and this is Luhmann's crucial assertion, legal programmes are always so-called *conditional programmes* (2004: 196). This type of programmes is structured strictly around an 'if ..., then ...' schemata. *If* I violate this legal norm, *then* I can expect that specific sanction. By clearly stipulating the legal effects of a various forms of action, the legal system employs these conditional programmes to carry out its societal function, i.e. to stabilise normative expectations and thereby provide a time binding between the present and the future. Luhmann even contends that this time-binding ability, where the system can use its conditional programmes to react to future situations without knowing them in detail in advance, makes it warranted to 'see law as a kind of *immunization system of society*. [...] The legal system makes no prognosis about when conflicts will happen, what the particular situation will be, who will be involved and how strong their involvement will be'; and yet, it provides ways of handling such future conflicts (2004: 171, italics added). It might be added that, just as an immunity system of an organism needs to be attacked to develop and reproduce itself, so the legal system depends on these conflicts in order to reproduce itself (2004: 477).

It should be noted, finally, that, similar to other social systems, law is an autopoietic, self-referential system. It is the legal system itself which determines its programmes and hence the regulation of its binary code. Clearly, law is tightly coupled to the political system, as I shall come back to below. For example, politicians may decide that toys must not contain any dangerous, potentially cancer-inducing chemicals. This is a political, collectively binding decision. Yet it is only when this decision is recognised by the legal system that it acquires a legal form. So the political decision becomes a legal reality only when it is transformed into law by the legal system, i.e. when it is enacted and enforced in the legal domain. Moreover, there is no guarantee that the legal transformation of the political decision occurs as the political system expected. It might be, for example, that the political wish to regulate the market for toys conflicts with laws on free market competition. Whether this is the case, and what legal consequences this might trigger, is an entirely legal, not political, matter of concern.[12]

## The economic system

Understanding the societal status of the economy constitutes a prominent sociological field of research that dates back to Marx and Weber, and which has been revitalised since the mid-1980s with the emergence of the so-called 'new economic sociology'. One of the significant contributions to this renewed sociological interest in the economy is Mark Granovetter's famous paper on 'Economic Action and Social Structure: The Problem of Embeddedness' (Granovetter 1985). Granovetter's argument is, briefly put, that economic action and social relations do not constitute distinct entities or domains. Rather economic action must be seen as embedded in social (interpersonal) relations. As he puts it, 'there is evidence all around us of the extent to which business relations are mixed up with social ones' (1985: 405). Luhmann's approach is very different and also much more radical. On the one hand, he would subscribe fully to the embeddedness thesis in the sense that, for Luhmann, it would be absurd to consider the economic domain as something non-social. On the other hand, he would be highly critical of the lack of differentiation between the social in general and the economic more specifically which Granovetter tends to posit. More specifically, what Luhmann would find neglected in Granovetter is an attentiveness to how the economy as a social phenomenon is differentiated from other social realms. Luhmann therefore goes in a different direction. For him, the economy is one of several function systems in society, differentiated from the systems of law, politics, art, etc. through its distinctive operational logic.[13]

According to Luhmann, the fundamental preoccupation of the economy is the problem of scarcity, which must be understood as a temporal problem. Both goods and money are scarce resources. If I eat my apple today, I cannot also eat it tomorrow. Similarly, if I spend my money today, I cannot spend it again tomorrow. This is quite basic and it means that, because of scarcity, 'the satisfaction of future needs must be treated as a present problem' (1982b: 195). Against this background, Luhmann says, the function of the economy is, 'under the condition of scarcity, to ensure future supply' (1997a: 758). Or more crudely, the function of the economic system is to regulate scarcity (1988b: 64–5).

Previously the economic system was organised around property with the corresponding code of having/not-having. Yet in the modern economy money constitutes the system's symbolically generalised medium of communication. Money is an extremely flexible medium that can be applied in all sorts of situations and without being affected, as it were, by its owner (1982b: 207). Money has the same value independently of whose hands it is in. Also, money does not pay attention to the motives behind its use; it can be used by gangsters to bribe politicians and by old ladies to buy biscuits for their visitors. As this indicates, money serves to mediate payments which, on their side, regulate scarcity. According to Luhmann, in the economy, 'the ultimate communication that composes the system, the one that cannot be broken down any further, is payment' (1995g: 461). Payments are fully self-referential operations. They enable new payments and are themselves only possible on the basis of previous payments (1988b: 52). The scarcity of money also applies to payments, however, and this is captured by the binary code of the economic system: payment/non-payment. The economic system employs this code to observe the world. Everything is divided into whether it can effect a payment which can produce new payments in the future (connecting communications). As Luhmann puts it, '[t]o pay or not to pay – that is, quite seriously, the question by which the existence of the economy is determined' (1989a: 52).

The code of payment/non-payment does not itself prescribe the correct use of its two sides. Therefore programmes are invented that can regulate the use of the code. The economic system's basic programme is that of prices since they 'permit a rapid determination of whether payments are right or not' (1989a: 53; see also 1988b: Ch. 1). If the computer costs €700, and I only have €500, then no payment can be effected. Other economic programmes include investment programmes as well as liquidity assessment programmes. The former define premises for whether, for example, investments (payments) should be placed in this or that stock. The latter regulate payments with a view to their effects on liquidity and credit flows (1988b: 250).

## The other function systems

In addition to the political, legal and economic systems, Luhmann has examined five other function systems in depth. One is the system of *art* the function of which is to provide society with new ways of observing itself by pointing to an imaginary order and '*demonstrating the compelling forces of order in the realm of the possible*' (2000a: 148, italics in original). The binary coding guiding the system of art is beautiful/ugly, although this code might be employed in other variations such as, for instance, provocative/appeasing. The programmes used by the art system to select its code values include manifests and styles (2000a: 234–5). The system's medium is art, which can be expressed in the form of paintings, sculptures, installations, etc. The system of *science* has already been touched upon in this chapter. The system's function is to generate new knowledge. Science operates through the symbolically generalised medium of truth and through the binary code, true/false. Its programmes consist of theories and methods (Luhmann 1990a).

The function of the system of *mass media* is to contribute 'towards society's construction of reality. Part of this includes a constant reactualization of the self-description of society and its cognitive world horizons' (Luhmann 2000e: 103). In other words, the mass media provide society with a continuous update on what society knows and how it describes and understands itself. As Luhmann says, '[w]hatever we know about our society, or indeed about the world in which we live, we know through the mass media' (2000e: 1). Luhmann does not define a specific symbolically generalised medium of communication for the mass media, but Hans-Georg Moeller has argued that 'public opinion' is the medium through which the mass media operate (Moeller 2006: 137). The binary code of the mass media is information/non-information where information is understood on basis of Bateson's previously mentioned definition as a difference that makes a difference. This means, quite simply, that the mass media cannot bring old news. As soon as something has been observed as information, it automatically turns into non-information, i.e. into something that no longer makes a difference. The programmes used by the mass media to select which side of the code is right include news (subdivided into conflicts, local relevance, norm violations, etc.), advertising and entertainment.

The no less than ambitious function of the system of *education* is to change people so at to prepare them for the communication that takes place in society (1995c; 2002b). More specifically, this system aims to change psychic systems: how people think. This is also why, according to Luhmann, the system of education has no symbolically generalised medium of communication. The system does not aim directly to make certain social experiences and actions more probable, but is focused on promoting specific patterns of thinking. Yet, the system does have a binary code which is to perform better or worse. This is measured, for instance, in grades. The programmes of the system consist above all in curricula and readings. For example, if a student can only account for 10 per cent of the readings at an exam, then he or she does not pass.

Finally, the function of the system of *religion* is to translate the indeterminacy of the world into a meaningful order (2000c: 127). The binary code of religion is immanence/transcendence, and at least in a Christian context the system's programmes are constituted by the rules set out in the Holy Scripture (1989a: 96). Similar to the system of education, religion has no fixed symbolically generalised medium of communication, although faith might be a candidate (2000c: 205–6).

These are the systems that Luhmann has analysed systematically. In addition to these he has suggested that a couple of other specific types of communication have been differentiated. One is intimate communication, centred on the symbolically generalised medium of love and typically organised in families or equivalents hereto (1990i; 1998a). Likewise, a medical code has emerged which distinguishes between sick and healthy and which guides the entire domain of treatment and cure (1990h).

## SOCIETAL INTEGRATION AND THE RELATIONS
## BETWEEN FUNCTION SYSTEMS

As mentioned at the beginning of this chapter, Luhmann's reflections on functional differentiation are articulated within the horizon of a broader sociological discussion of societal differentiation. This naturally raises the question of how, more specifically, Luhmann's analysis relates to the existing literature. What similarities and differences can be identified between Luhmann's theory of functional differentiation and the diagnoses put forward by scholars from Marx onward? Needless to say, no full analysis of the various sociological theories of differentiation can be presented here (see for this purpose Schimank 1996). A few selected observations will have to suffice.

To begin with, there seems to be at least one interesting parallel between Marx and Luhmann. Although Marx's terminology was entirely different he also described the economy as a domain characterised by its own specific logics. Indeed, it was one of Marx' central ideas that the capitalist economy is founded on self-regulating practices and logics. In a sense, Luhmann appropriates this image of the self-organising economy and extends it to other societal domains (law, politics, art, etc.). This expansion of the self-organising logic at the same time suggests what constitutes Luhmann's main objection to Marx' work. Thus, argues Luhmann, the Marxist assertion that modern society is founded on its economic structure severely overestimates the importance of the economy vis-à-vis other domains:

> In the definition of society as a whole in economic terms, what is lacking [...] above all is a sufficient appreciation for parallel phenomena in different functional areas. Missing is a basis for comparing systems and for distilling abstract characteristics of modernity, which can be found in more or less all functions systems.
>
> (Luhmann 1998b: 9)

Bluntly put, what Luhmann proposes is that Marx simply stopped short. He did not take the full consequences of his own analysis but falsely assumed that the internal logics he identified in the economy applied to the economy alone.[14]

Working in the Marxist tradition, but reformulating it fundamentally, Pierre Bourdieu has espoused a theory of differentiation which suggests that society is divided into a number of fields (art, economy, education, etc.), each of which is characterised by its autonomous modes of operation. This is at first sight rather similar to what Luhmann claims, and the two sociologists do share certain interests and observations. For example, as Georg Kneer (2004: 40–1) rightly notes, both Luhmann and Bourdieu formulate their differentiation theories in a way that allows for comparison between systems (Luhmann) or fields (Bourdieu). But there are also crucial differences. Among other things, Bourdieu assumes a struggle and hierarchy within the fields; Luhmann sees nothing of this in function systems. Also, the functional aspect of differentiation that Luhmann stresses plays hardly any role for Bourdieu who also does not share Luhmann's attention to binary codes (for further differences, see Nassehi and Nollmann 2004).

While Luhmann has only relatively little in common with Marxist and neo-Marxist scholars, one might presume instead that he continues in the footsteps of Durkheim and the latter's analysis of division of labour as being the defining feature of modern society. This impression is only emphasised by the fact that Durkheim was a key proponent of the functionalist path of sociology that Luhmann would later pursue and take in new directions. Moreover, Durkheim is one of only very few scholars (alongside Weber, Parsons and Spencer-Brown) to whom Luhmann devoted independent articles or chapters. For example, Luhmann wrote the introduction to a German edition of Durkheim's *Division of labor* (Luhmann 1982a). However, in spite of the Durkheimian influences that might be detected in Luhmann's work, it would be misleading to see his theory of functional differentiation as a mere modernised version of Durkheim's argument on the division of labour. The latter evokes an image of society as constituting a unity, which is divided into a number of parts, and where this division is based on an idea of specialisation (à la 'if the economist does this, the scientist can specialise in that') as the foundation for mutual exchange and common benefits. As compared to this Durkheimian notion of division of labour, Luhmann's account of functional differentiation presents a far more radical view on society (e.g. 1995e: 20; 1997a: 761).

Thus, rather than being concerned with how different parts of society specialise in different kinds of labour, the kind of differentiation Luhmann analyses has a much more epistemological character. The function systems simply employ different *contextures*, as Luhmann says, drawing on the work of Gotthard Günther (e.g. Günther 1979). In Luhmann's rendering of Günther, contexture (one of Günther's key notions) refers to the world view or rationality that guides how function systems approach the world. Each function system is mono-contextural because it observes the world through its specific two-valued contexture, the binary code, and everything is excluded from sight which does not fit into one of the contexture's two values. In other words, Luhmann's notion of functional differentiation refers to a differentiation, not of specialised forms of labour, but rather of fundamentally different, non-congruent perspectives on the reality. So when modern society is seen as being differentiation into systems of science, economy, etc., the point is not that this division is driven by a functional division of labour where the economy can specialise in economic matters because science takes care of scientific matters, and vice versa. Rather this differentiation enacts a separation of contexts: science approaches the world through the code true/false, whereas the economy observes the world through its code, payment/non-payment.

Given this differentiation of contexts, Luhmann describes modern society as having a 'poly-contextural structure' where 'it is impossible to bring two different contextualities into an immediate confrontation' (Günther 1979: 288). The function systems simply speak different languages; they approach the world on basis of different horizons – this is one of Luhmann's chief sociological observations. While this image of functional differentiation as a basically poly-contextural reality differs markedly from Durkheim's idea of a division of labour, it comes close, as Uwe Schimank has observed, to Weber's idea of a differentiation of value spheres (Schimank 1996: 156). Similar to Luhmann, Weber's account essentially refers to how modern society is differentiated into a series of independent, incongruent perspectives or rationalities.[15] Contrary to Luhmann, however, Weber does not link this observation to the idea of a differentiation of binary codes, such as the notion of contextures implies.

The difference between a division of labour argument and the diagnosis of polycontexturality raises an important question of how the functionally differentiated systems relate to one another. More specifically, whereas the interrelation between societal subsystems follows neatly from the division of labour idea, the possible interconnections are far less obvious when differentiation takes a polycontextural form. How do the systems of science, economy, politics, law, religion, etc. relate to one another, given their incongruent perspectives/contextures/rationalities? In Luhmann's account the answer to this question becomes an answer to a classical sociological problem, namely what integrates a differentiated society? The problem of integration was central to Durkheim who believed in the emergence of a new organic solidarity which holds the modern divided society together. Luhmann follows an entirely different line of reasoning. According to Luhmann, there is no underlying solidarity. Nor is modern society based on common values that ensure integration in the light of differentiation. Quite the contrary, Luhmann argues, it is crucial finally to go beyond these, in his view, old-fashioned presuppositions. First of all, classical notions of integration revolve around the problem of how the whole and its parts are related (this is the case in both Durkheim and Parsons, see Luhmann 1997a: 602). The theoretical movement Luhmann enacts from whole/part to system/environment reformulates the problem of integration. So does, secondly, the diagnosis of functional differentiation, which presents the problem of integration in a radically new guise.

Thus, Luhmann states, in a functionally differentiated society, integration does not refer to the overall societal level (i.e. to what used to be conceptualised as the whole), but rather to the interrelations between function systems. More specifically, integration is defined by Luhmann as 'the reduction of the degrees of freedom of subsystems' (1997a: 603; see also 2002a: 338; 2004: 489).[16] According to this understanding, integration refers to how the self-regulation of functional subsystems is conditioned or limited by other function systems. The integration of two systems is greater, the fewer options the one system has because of the other system's limitation of its selectivity. On this view, states Luhmann, both cooperation and, especially, conflict are examples of integration (1997a: 604; 2002a: 338). A conflict between two systems produces a particularly strong kind of integration where each of the systems must be very attentive to what the other system does (what resources it uses, what strategies it employs, etc.). As this shows, integration is not to be found in 'the relation of the "parts" to a "whole"', but rather in the flexible, also historically flexible, adjustments of subsystems to one another' (1997a: 604). Luhmann is careful to stress that, according to this understanding, integration is 'no value-laden concept and it also is not "better" than disintegration' (1997a: 604). There is no normative content hidden in Luhmann's use of the concept; it merely refers to a specific intersystemic relation (see also 1990c: 422–3). In fact, states Luhmann counter-intuitively, since conflicts are a sign of integration, it is important for 'a complex society to provide sufficient disintegration' (1997a: 604). This understanding of integration does not contradict the whole autopoietic framework. Function systems are and remain autopoietic, operationally closed systems, but they may develop ties that limit one another's elbowroom.

Luhmann proposes several concepts to understand such integrations between function systems. The most important ones are performances and structural couplings. While structural couplings is a general notion to describe how systems relate to their environment (including systems in their environment), performances refer, as previously mentioned, to the specific contributions that function systems provide for one another. For example, the performance of the legal system is to solve conflicts, whereas the economic system's performance is to satisfy needs.

Just as the various performances cannot be determined theoretically, but must be studied empirically, so structural couplings between function systems must be examined according to how they appear as empirical phenomena. Due to the large number of function systems, one can expect a lot of structural couplings. Among the important couplings that Luhmann analyses are those between *politics and economy*. For example, these two systems are coupled through taxes: the political system is dependent on collecting taxes for fulfilling its promises (1997a: 781; 2000b: 385–6). Another coupling between the two systems is that of central banks which can print money. In both cases, the political system is dependent on this access to the economic system. Yet this 'access' remains a structural coupling rather than a mutual operational intrusion, because even if the money/taxes are used for specific political purposes, they follow the dynamics of the economic system once they are sent out in economic circulation.

Similarly, the *law and politics* are structurally coupled through constitutions (2004: 403–12). Constitutions couple the two systems by ensuring that, even if the political system makes new laws, the legal system is free to make decisions according to legal rather than political objectives and procedures (a separation of powers). Further, *law and economy* are structurally coupled through contracts and property. The fact that the economy can rely on the legal system to enforce contracts and property rights enables economic parties who do not know one another to engage in all sorts of transactions (1997a: 784; 2004: 390–402). And should contracts and property rights be violated, then recourse can be made to the legal system which will use its legal decision-making in the particular conflict to reproduce itself.

While the systems of law, politics and economy have built a number of structural couplings with one another as well as with other systems, some function systems are only loosely coupled to others. This is the case, not least, for the religious system which 'has hardly developed any structural couplings' (1997a: 787).

# 5

# Consequences of functional differentiation

Should one identify the two main sociological contributions of Luhmann, the most obvious candidates would be his conception of social systems as autopoietic, operationally closed systems of communication, on the one hand, and his diagnosis of modern society as being functionally differentiated, on the other. In the present chapter I wish to explore in more detail the consequences of functional differentiation. I will begin by examining Luhmann's assertion that functional differentiation leads to a de-centring of society. This discussion will contain an outlook to some of the normative underpinnings of the theory of functional differentiations, and it will show that Luhmann does not lament the de-centring that functional differentiation entails. Quite the opposite, he is convinced that the accomplishments of modern society have been achieved, not in spite of this de-centring of society, but rather because of it. At the same time, the lack of a centre also produces a number of challenges. This will be illustrated through Luhmann's analyses of risks and ecological dangers. These parts of Luhmann's work depict modern society as almost incapable of addressing grand societal challenges: since there is no centre of society, there is no system that can credibly assume responsibility for dealing with society's grand problems and direct the other systems accordingly.

The functional differentiation of modern society therefore creates a structural barrier to solving great challenges. The disillusionment this might give rise to is only likely to increase when turning to Luhmann's analyses of inclusion and exclusion, to be discussed at the end of the chapter. Here Luhmann indicates that the functional differentiation, which is so precious to him, might be subdued to a new mode of differentiation in the future, namely one which pivots around the inclusion/exclusion distinction, and which makes survival a pressing issue in the zones of exclusion.

## A DE-CENTRED SOCIETY

Luhmann's assertion that functional differentiation enacts a strict separation between the various function systems, which organise their operations according to purely internal, code-guided criteria, has several crucial dimensions and implications. First of all, the emergence of this mode of societal differentiation has radically suspended a geographic division of systems. The economic system operates world-wide and financial markets in one part of the world are intimately linked to those in other parts. Likewise, the system of science functions globally. The assessment of true and false is not subjected to local prejudices but follow global standards. And although the political system describes itself in a state semantics, which suggests that the system operates within clearly defined nation-state boundaries, the political system is also globally integrated. Political developments in one country can have significant ramifications on politics in other countries (e.g. who is elected president in the USA; which fraction is having the upper hand in Iran, etc.). Consequently, Luhmann argues, modern society has developed into a *world society* (1990m; 1997a: 145–71). 'The inclusion of all communicative behavior into one societal system is the unavoidable consequence of functional differentiation. Using this form of differentiation, society becomes a global system', meaning also that it does not make sense to speak of society as divided into regional and territorially limited entities (1990m: 178). This does not suggest, for example, that politics in Finland is just as important, on a global scale, as US American politics. The world society thesis merely states that no independent nation-state politics is possible; every nation-state political system is embedded in a global system of politics.

Second, in addition to being a world society the functional differentiation produces an image of a flat, non-hierarchical society. No system can intervene in the operations of other function systems, and no function system is per definition more important than the others. In Luhmann's own words, 'a society which is structured according to function systems has *no central agency*. It is a society without an *apex* or *center*' (1990d: 31, italics in original). Consequently, he contends (reversing a classic Aristotelian dictum), in the modern society 'the whole is less than the sum of its parts' (1982c: 238). There is simply no collective adding up of perspectives, but rather a differentiation into singular horizons.

This idea that no function system has primacy over the others is a claim that sets Luhmann's theory radical apart from many other socio-logical positions. Most significantly, of course, this assertion of the a-centric society conflicts sharply with Marxist approaches that stress the allegedly central role the economy plays in the final analysis. Luhmann does not buy into this idea of the economy forming the basis of society. Nor does he accept the idea, often suggested by the mass media and by politicians, that the political system constitutes the core of society, the centre from which all other systems are directed. Quite the contrary, Luhmann's diagnosis of the modern functionally differenti-ated society leaves rather little room for politics. And calls for revolu-tionary action have become wholly archaic: 'it is not possible to make revolution any more. There is no aim, no objective, no centre, or no top of the system which you could eliminate and then you would have a good society' (Luhmann 1994b: 4). Not only does the idea of the polit-ical system's primacy conflict with the functionally differentiated reality of modern society, Luhmann believes; when the idea is put forward as a normative ideal, it even shakes the foundation for modern society.

Thus, any call for centring society around one system, be it politics, the economy, science or whatever, poses a threat to what Luhmann sees as the most significant achievement of functional differentiation, namely that it represents a radical contrast to totalitarianism. Whereas totalitari-anism is characterised by centring society on one or few systems (often politics or religion), with all the associated misfortunes (e.g. lack of inde-pendence and functional specialisation), a functionally differentiated society accepts the independence of the systems and uses this feature as a resource, not only for purposes of specialisation, but also as a democratic resource. Indeed, Luhmann writes in one of normative considerations, it is in the end modern democracy which is at stake in discussions about functional differentiation:

> One of the basic questions concerning the theoretical and political orientation of the present is therefore whether one can tolerate the idea of a centerless society and see in this the conditions for an effective, democratic politics. Or whether, in view of the entire situation of the system of society, one believes one can or even has to attribute a central responsibility to politics that might possibly destroy its present boundaries and the laborious procedures of the democratic determination of opinions. The present theoretical diagnosis [i.e. Luhmann's, CB] answers this question in the first

sense. One cannot functionally differentiate society in such a way as to make politics its center without destroying society.

(1990d: 32–3)

So for Luhmann, democracy as we know it is only possible on the basis of a functionally differentiated society. This is why Luhmann is so critical against attempts to loosen the boundaries between function systems, for such loosening amounts to a de-differentiation and therefore leads society away from the conditions supporting its democratic structure – and towards more totalitarian forms. This will be further discussed in Chapter 6.

One important consequence of this diagnosis of the de-centred society is that there is no central perspective from which to observe social phenomena. Each function system applies its own particular observational frame, its binary code, and there is no way of harmonising the incongruent lenses. They simply have different prescriptions.[1] As a result, the same phenomenon is observed entirely different by the various function systems. 'Society remains the same but appears different depending upon the functional subsystem (politics, economy, science, mass media, education, religion, art, and so on) that describes it. The same is different' (Luhmann 1995f: 48).

For example, a financial crisis is observed by the economic system in terms of how it affects payments. More specifically, a financial crisis is likely to influence the programmes used by the economic system. For instance, investment programmes and liquidity programmes are modified so as to ensure that banks lend less money that can be used as payments for consumption, thereby impeding circulation in the economic system. In the political system, the crisis is observed according to the government/opposition code, so that the opposition might blame the government for having stimulated, or at least not prevented, the crisis. The government, by contrast, might attribute the crisis to market failure rather than political laxness and show political determination by claiming stronger regulation of financial markets. The scientific system might be largely unaffected by the crisis and merely observe it in terms of the effects it has on funding possibilities. For example, research proposals might flourish which address the conditions and effects of financial crises. The religious system might see an opportunity for demonstrating the supremacy of religious values (as compared to the pursuit of ephemeral economic gains), and for showing that religious services might offer consolidation for those who are negatively affected by the crisis.

As said, the key point is that the same phenomenon, here a financial crisis, appears entirely different – and hence with completely different connecting communications – in the different function systems. Had Luhmann not been so critical of ontological frameworks, one might have said that the function systems produce each their ontology, each their reality, and that the functionally differentiated society therefore embodies multiple ontologies.

This incompatibility of perspectives is buttressed by a temporal dimension, which adds a further layer to the diagnosis of the de-centred society. Just as there is no central vantage point in the functionally differentiated society, so there is no central watch, so to speak. The function systems are organised around different temporal horizons, meaning that modern society has no common time frame, no synchro-nised time. For example, the political system's temporal structure is organised around electoral terms (usually four to five years). As a conse-quence, the political system is likely to refrain from collective decisions that have a longer time perspective. One example is climate politics which is made difficult not only because it has to transcend nation-state boundaries to be effective (thereby having to confront all sorts of national rather than global interests), it must also overcome the struc-tural problem that effective long run measures cannot easily be used to evaluate the performance of politicians in the short run. There is, in other words, a temporal barrier confronting climate politics, and indeed any policy field, where politicians are likely to focus on measures which can produce political results that are popular here and now rather than effective in the long run.

By contrast, the system of science has a much longer temporal horizon which cannot be broken down into electoral time periods. In science, it might take a decade of meticulous efforts to reach a break-through which is evaluated positively by one's peers and hence by the system. The economic system is confronted with much shorter time frames. Most significantly, in financial markets seconds can be decisive for success or failure. Likewise, the mass media operate with a short time horizon. This is an effect if the very code of the system, information/non-information. 'Information cannot be repeated; as soon as it becomes an event, it becomes non-information. A news item run twice might still have its meaning, but it loses its information value' (Luhmann 2000e: 19). Since the mass media cannot reproduce the news, it has to invent new information all the time, putting the system under constant time pressure.

The key implication of the lacking central perspective and the missing synchronicity of modern society is that there is no way to regulate or coordinate measures across function systems. Since the observational and temporal horizons of the different function systems do not melt together, there is 'no central coordinating mechanism' to which we can make recourse in order to meet the challenges that society faces (Luhmann 1994b: 4). Moreover, every function system can always only provide a partial solution, namely a solution which matches its specific logic. While this might be discomforting news, Luhmann insists that societal challenges are embedded in, and must be understood against the backdrop of, functional differentiation. Ignoring this functionally differentiated backcloth is like failing to acknowledge gravity: we can proceed as if it did not exist, but it keeps returning to leave its mark.

In the following sections I will examine how the de-centring affects modern society's ability to handle what are perceived by some observers as grand societal challenges. The first challenge to be discussed is that of risk.

## RISK SOCIETY

The notion of risk is intimately linked to another German sociologist, Ulrich Beck, and his famous diagnosis of risk society. This diagnosis was put forward most notably in the 1986 book *Risk Society*, and further elaborated in a series of subsequent publications (Beck 1992; 1994; 1995). Beck's argument is that modern society is currently undergoing a profound change. Whereas the industrial phase of modernity used to be concerned with the production and distribution of wealth, contemporary society is engaged in a simultaneous production and distribution of risks. To capture this, Beck states, 'the concept of risk society designates a stage of modernity in which the threats produced so far on the path of industrial society begin to predominate' (1994: 6). This is related to what Beck calls reflexive modernisation, which refers to modernisation's feedback onto itself: the important risks of today are not accidental, natural occurrences (e.g. the eruption of volcanoes), but rather systematically produced consequences of modernisation itself. Examples include the Chernobyl disaster, which occurred the same year as *Risk Society* was published, or flooding to the extent that it is a result of humanly induced global warming. For Beck, such examples illustrate that the success of modernity now begins to undermine, or at least threaten, society. That is, these and similar examples show that, due to the advanced state that modern society has reached (within science, technology, etc.), it produces highly incalculable results with far-reaching equally incalculable negative effects.

Beck's analysis has gained wide popularity because it is able to capture phenomena that have received much attention in recent years, including genetically modified food and climate change – both of which can be seen as examples of how the risks that society is confronted with are produced systemically by society itself. Luhmann has also addressed the problem of risk. His most important publications on the topic date back to the early 1990s where he wrote an article and subsequently a book on the topic (Luhmann 1990g; 1993d). At that time, Beck's diagnosis had already received immense popular as well as scholarly interest. Although risk has been discussed by many others prior to Beck, it is likely that Luhmann was provoked by the popularity Beck's examination enjoyed to develop his own contribution to the debate (for an account of various sociological analyses of risk, see Arnoldi 2009). However, while it is clear that Beck forms part of that branch of sociological thinking that Luhmann's analysis seeks to go beyond (see 1993d: 5), Beck does not assume a central place in Luhmann's writings on risk, at least not on an explicit level.

Luhmann's investigation makes two central points. First, on a conceptual level, Luhmann follows his Spencer-Brownian inspiration and examines risk as a two-sided form: if risk constitutes the one side of a two-sided form, then what is at the other side? As mentioned in Chapter 3, it makes a great difference for any concept how it is defined through its other, presently unmarked side. According to Luhmann, it is often assumed that risk is constituted conceptually by the notion of security, expressed as risk⌐security (1993d: 19). The underlying message conveyed by this distinction is that if only the risks be reduced or removed, a state of security will ensue. While this might be a politically convenient way of understanding risk because risk/security is easily transferred into a government/opposition distinction ('the government does not address the risks we face; chose us, the opposition, instead, and we will ensure security'), not much is gained sociologically-analytically by conceiving risk as being opposed to security, argues Luhmann. The reason is that since both risk and security refer to an unknown future, it is not possible to guarantee future security. One can never be sure that this or that action will provide future security. Therefore, '[s]ecurity as a counterconcept to risk remains an empty concept in this constellation' (1993d: 20).

Consequently, Luhmann suggests that risk be defined through a different counterconcept. Specifically, he proposes to distinguish between *risk and danger.* Luhmann admits that the notions of risk and danger seem so close to one another that it makes little sense to treat them as opposites. Yet, he maintains, upon closer inspection risk and danger are disparate, namely with respect to how they relate to decision making. He thus speaks of risk when the possible damages of a system are attributed to decisions made by the system itself. Dangers, by contrast, refer to damages to the system that are not attributed to the system's decisions. For example, if I speculate all my savings in stocks, this designates a risk because the loss of money I may suffer in a bear (downward) market can be attributed to my investment decision. By contrast, if a person loses his or her job as a side effect of economic recession, then this is a danger since the negative effects cannot be attributed to the person's decisions. Put differently, risks refer to decisions that could have been different (instead of speculating in stocks, I could have kept my money under the pillow or put it in the bank), whereas dangers refer to damages that one is simply exposed to. The example illustrates another general point. What appears as a risk for one person may be a danger for someone else (1993d: 108–9). Heavily geared investments in the financial markets (*risk*) might trigger a financial collapse which has negative effects on people who did not speculate (*danger*).

Luhmann admits that, obviously, the behaviour of those who are exposed to dangers 'also has a part to play, *but only in the sense of it placing people in a situation in which loss or damage occurs*' (1993d: 23, italics added). This suggests that there are borderline cases where it is not always easy to say if a risk or a danger is at hand. For example, if I am mugged during a trip to Sao Paolo, then this could be analysed as a danger: strolling quietly about, I was simply in a situation where the loss occurred. Yet the robbery may also be analysed as a risk since Sao Paolo is famous for its high crime rates, meaning that the decision to go there (and not to, for instance, Nice or Amsterdam) entails a high likelihood of being robbed. According to this interpretation, the loss inferred as a result of the robbery can be attributed to my decision to travel to a place with high crime rates.

Luhmann's second important point is that if risks are seen as damages, losses, etc. that are attributed to decisions, then nothing per se is a risk. Risk is and remains a specific kind of attribution, i.e. something that an observer installs. To return to the example above, it depends on the observer whether the mugging in Sao Paolo constitutes a risk or a danger. This has the crucial implication that Luhmann's analysis refines the diagnosis of risk society put forward by Beck. From Luhmann's perspective, it does not make sense to speak of modern society as entering a phase where risk becomes a predominant characteristic in the sense that the fundamental dynamics in contemporary society are now organised around risk production and distribution. Instead, Luhmann continues along the lines of his turn to second-order observation and asks how various observers observe through the distinction between risk and danger. How do they apply this distinction and with what consequences?

This approach might show that the risk/danger distinction is being used more often than before and that it guides more communication than previously. On this view, a revised notion of risk society is meaningful from a Luhmannian perspective, insofar as it designates a tendency *where societal observers begin to observe society's problems according to the risk/danger distinction* – and more specifically, by indicating the risk side of that distinction. But this says nothing about whether the relation between decisions and perceived damages is 'real' (that the latter do in fact depend on specific decisions), only that this is how the relation is observed.

In continuation of this, Luhmann's analysis suggests that risk communication might be subject to self-perpetuating dynamics, which buttress the tendency toward ever more risk communication. In the political system, the opposition may blame the government for doing too little in terms of addressing perceived risks (for instance, health risks). This might induce the government to grant more money to science, arguing that it is science not politics that produces the kind of knowledge which is needed in order to manage risks effectively. Yet producing more knowledge is likely to generate new types of risks. For example, when it is demonstrated scientifically that smoking or the consumption of specific types of fat food have negative health effects, then smoking and consumption of this food are transformed into risk behaviours. When people smoke cigarettes or eat fatty food, they make a decision (they could have refrained from this behaviour), and future damages that may result from this behaviour can therefore be attributed to the decision. The more general effect is that what is intended politically as a tool for managing risks results, in this example, in novel scientifically produced risks, which raise new demands on the political system, and so it can go on.

Importantly, as this shows, and this is one of the key features separating Luhmann from Beck, Luhmann's analysis of risk is unfolded within the framework of functional differentiation. That is, Luhmann does not suggest that modern society is adopting a fundamentally new form. To be sure, risk semantics might become still more prominent, meaning that ever more phenomena are observed on basis of the risk/danger distinction. But on a societal level, these observations continue to be structured by some more fundamental distinctions, namely the binary codes of the function systems. This means that risk communication takes different forms in the various function systems, according to what the individual systems' logics prescribe. The de-centring of society therefore implies that risk attributions are likely to differ markedly across the function systems. For example, in the political system, risk communication revolves around the division between government and opposition and is translated into a question of getting more votes. In the mass media, by contrast, risk communication is translated into a question of whether it can be sold as news or not. The media cannot keep reporting about the same risk, but need to renew their focus again and again, changing the focus to other risks or to entirely different topics (sport results, weather forecasts, new travel destinations, etc.). The risks that the political system might be concerned with, and which might attract temporary media attention, may play no role in the economic system. It might be, for example, that both the political system and the mass media are preoccupied with the risks allegedly associated with a particular product (e.g. cigarettes). However, in the economic system this only matters to the extent that it affects the sales.

Relatedly, due to the functional de-centring of modern society, there is no place in society from which to enact a coordinated regulation of observed risks. While a financial crisis might be viewed in risk terms in the political and the economic systems, their different logics obstruct any synchronised action. The economy cannot suddenly begin to deal semi-politically with risks, and vice versa. The economic system can only approach risks economically, the political system can only attack them politically, etc.

To repeat the underlying point, for Luhmann, risk communication does not suspend or replace functional differentiation; risk should be analysed instead with respect to how it is unfolded vis-à-vis the binary logics of the functional differentiated systems. It follows from this that, drawing on Luhmann's distinction between societal structure and semantics, 'risk society', as Luhmann sees it, does not refer to a change in the societal structure (functional differentiation), but rather to the emergence of a new semantics, a new vocabulary with which society describes itself (see also 1997a: 1088–96). This self-description may be prominent at the moment, but it has to compete with a plethora of other self-descriptions, such as the 'network society' (Castells 1996) and the 'experience society' (Schulze 1992). And it does not set the logic of functional differentiation aside.

## ECOLOGICAL COMMUNICATION

In Beck's work, contemporary risk society is often (but not exclusively) illustrated through ecological risks. Luhmann, on his side, treats risks and ecological matters in different contexts. Interestingly, his main contribution to the discussion of ecological challenges was published the same year as Beck's book on the *Risk Society* appeared, namely in

1986. Luhmann's contribution, a book entitled *Ecological Communication* and subtitled in the German original: *Can Modern Society Adjust Itself to the Exposure to Ecological Dangers?*, was based on a talk he held in 1985, and it therefore actually precedes Beck's analysis. The conclusions the two sociologists reach are very different. As intimated above, Beck voices a clearly critical position that emphasises the problems relating to the alleged magnitude and systemic constitution of the current risks. Luhmann's starting point is different. He begins with the difference between system and environment, here the system of *society* and its environment. On this basis he excavates how society is able to respond to ecological challenges.

It is by no means obvious how such a response could be conceived. After all, it follows from the strict separation between system and environment and from the definition of society as the sum of communication that '[s]ociety cannot communicate *with* but only *about* its environment' (1989a: 117, italics in original). How to discuss a societal response to ecological dangers on that background? Luhmann's way of approaching this problem goes through the notion of *resonance*, which refers to situations where occurrences in the environment trigger some effect in the system. Given the assumption that social systems are autopoietic, operationally closed systems, resonance is an improbable occurrence. Also, the operationally closed nature of social systems means that resonance will always be very selective; it has to be filtered through the operational modus of the system in question. Be that as it may, Luhmann believes that '[w]e can formulate the question of the ecological basis of and danger to social life much more exactly if we look for the conditions under which the states and changes in the social environment *find resonance* within society' (1989a: 16, italics in original). Crucially, however, the de-centring of society means that it does not speak with one voice. Society is no unity and it can have no unitary approach to ecological challenges. Instead the differentiation into a series of function systems implies that society's resonance to ecological dangers must be examined on the level of function systems.

Yet when looking into how function systems display resonance to ecological problems it appears that they do so entirely uncoordinated and according to purely 'local' or system-specific criteria. For example, since the political system organises its communication around the government/opposition code, ecological problems only matter to the system insofar as they can be translated into the logics of this code. The opposition might hold the government responsible for increasing pollution; the government might respond by pointing to recent initiatives or by displacing the blame, arguing that it is the economy which is ignorant toward ecological problems. In any case, this need not produce measures that lead to any substantial engagement with ecological issues; in fact, this is very improbable, as I shall come back to.

Due to the high degree of selectiveness on the side of function systems, society 'brings *too little resonance* into play for the exposure to ecological dangers' (1989a: 116, italics in original). At the same time, Luhmann argues, one might point to an even bigger problem, namely that of '*too much resonance*' (1989a: 116, italics in original). This problem refers not so much to the resonance between society and its environment, but rather to the resonances or interdependencies between function systems. According to Luhmann,

> Even if the function systems are differentiated according to their own autopoiesis, codes and programs, they can be disturbed by communication in a way that is entirely different from the way society itself relates to its environment. It is therefore highly probable that turbulences of one function system are transferred to others even if, and because, each proceeds according to its own specific code.
>
> (1989a: 117)

Luhmann illustrates this by referring to how the economic system becomes dependent on science once it begins to rely on the latter's developments. For example, the whole pharmacy industry would be seriously affected if it turned out that decades of research supporting this industry had been manipulated. Luhmann's crucial point is that these resonances between function systems are entirely incontrollable, partly because there is no place in the modern de-centred society from where intersystemic resonances could be governed, and partly because the autopoietic logic of each system can create very asymmetric effects. As Luhmann argues in an almost chaos-theoretical vein,

> Through resonance small changes in one system can trigger great changes in another. Payments of money to a politician that play no role in the economic process – measured by the hundreds of billions of dollars that are transferred back and forth daily – can become a political scandal.
>
> (1989a: 117)

This has huge implications for how society can respond to ecological dangers. To begin with, since society can only communicate about (and not with) its environment, there is no fixed procedure to make ecological dangers relevant to society. To be sure, green social movements as well as environmental scientists might claim to be spokespersons for the ecological environment or, more modestly, to provide knowledge about ecosystems. Yet whatever is communicated about ecological dangers, there is no guarantee that this will have any, much less the desired, effects on the relation between society and its environment. Just as society consists of autopoietic communication systems, so the environment consists of all sorts of (non-communicative) autopoietic systems to which communication has no direct access.

This refers back to the issue that was touched upon above. Whatever measures are taken by function systems, these are likely to have far bigger implications *within* society, i.e. with respect to intersystemic resonances, than for society's relation to its ecological environment. Granted, the political system may make collectively binding decisions about ecological matters. It may be decided, for instance, that only such and such $CO_2$ emission levels are allowed. Crucially, however, these decisions 'have no direct ecological, but only socially internal effects' (1989a: 119). For example, strict emission regulation in Europe may induce corporations to move their production to less regulated regions and countries, with negative effects on employment rates in Europe and with no sure net ecological gains. Similar to other social systems, therefore, the political system cannot solve ecological dangers, for it has no controlling access to society's environment. It can communicate about these dangers, but it is more probable that its communication will have unanticipated effects within society (due to intersystem relations) than it will improve society's relation to its environment. Society's environment simply cannot be determined politically (or, indeed, socially).

In spite of this, Luhmann acknowledges that the political system may be the natural 'place to start the business of addressing ecological issues' (1989a: 119). After all, grand problems are often addressed politically, and the political system may therefore 'function as a kind of continuous-flow heater', as Luhmann puts it (1989a: 120). One should bear in mind, however, that attributing to the political system the responsibility for handling ecological dangers may be a risky endeavour: as mentioned above, what might be 'politically convenient and acceptable solutions' to ecological dangers may lead to 'functional disturbances in other systems' (1989a: 120).

What Luhmann attempts to demonstrate in his analysis of ecological communication is that there are no easy solutions to ecological problems. More devastating, there are vast structural barriers to such solutions, these barriers being constituted not least by the functional differentiation of society and by society's communicative closure vis-à-vis its environment. It might be argued that Luhmann's analysis draws attention to a more general problem, namely the radical impotence of function systems to deal with omni-societal challenges, i.e. challenges that go across the boundaries of the singular function systems. A de-centred society has no obvious way of handling problems that are likely to be perceived entirely different in the different function systems. Does this leave us with no hope? Is there no way out of this gloomy picture of modern society's structural incapacity to deal with ecological issues? Luhmann's most positive solution consists in a call for social rationality, which would mean that 'the ecological difference of society and its external environment is reintroduced within society and used as its main difference' (1989a: 137). Yet, he offers no specific answer to how this re-entry procedure might be achieved in practice.

Here one might find help in Bruno Latour's work instead. Latour has argued for a new democratic order, a so-called 'parliament of things', in which especially ecological issues can be discussed in new ways (Latour 1993: 142–5; 2004). Briefly put, this new parliamentary structure should break down usual divisions between science and politics and bring representatives from both domains into dialogue. Latour mentions the 1997 Kyoto conference as a successful example of how this might be organised, for here 'politicians and scientists, industrialists and militants found themselves on the benches of the *same assembly*' (2004: 56, italics in original). In many respects Latour represents an entirely different perspective than that of Luhmann. For example, Latour does not operate with an image of society as being differentiated into a series of operationally closed function systems (Latour critiques Luhmann on several occasions in Latour 2005). Still, his suggestion of a parliament of things could be rephrased and understood in Luhmannian terms. Thus, in systems-theory terms, the Kyoto assembly that Latour refers to can be conceived as an attempt to form an *organisation* which is able to address omni-societal challenges, across the individual function systems' logics. As mentioned in Chapter 4, organisations can cross the divides between function systems and therefore offer a way for society to observe how its functional differentiation produces limits to societal problem management. Obviously, there is no guarantee that an organisation, in whatever form, can actually respond successfully to ecological dangers. Yet, from a Luhmannian point of view, one could hardly put faith in anything but organisations.

If Luhmann leaves only little redemption in his discussion of ecological dangers, this is not much different in his other discussions of the contemporary challenges that society faces. In particular, as I shall demonstrate in the following, the rather bleak prospects he outlines in the field of ecological communication are paralleled in his analyses of inclusion and exclusion.

## INCLUSION/EXCLUSION

Luhmann acknowledges that globalisation processes have produced vast changes *within* the function systems since World War II (1997a: 1143). But he does not support the claim that functional differentiation as such is being transformed or superseded. He therefore never hesitates to crit- icise the idea that society has advanced into a late or postmodern state (e.g. Bauman 1997; Lyotard 1984). For Luhmann, accounts of 'the so-called postmodern', as he puts it (1997a: 1143–9), fail to demonstrate that functional differentiation, and hence modernity, has actually been left behind. In other words, Luhmann does not believe that sociologists who claim that we live in a postmodern society succeed in showing that the structural order which characterises modernity has actually been suspended (1989a: 114–5; e.g. 1995h; 1997a: 1143–9). As the discussion of Beck's diagnosis of risk society demonstrated, Luhmann's critique not only applies to proponents of post or late modernity, but indeed to any claim that modern society, as with a stroke of the pen, has entered an entirely new phase.

That said, the turn to functional differentiation should not be misin- terpreted. For example, functional differentiation does not make other forms of differentiation obsolete. As Luhmann puts it, '[t]he different forms of system differentiation are not necessarily mutually exclusive' (1990c: 424). In fact, he claims, functional differentiation actually increases the likelihood that segmentary and stratificatory differentia- tions will (re)appear as a result of the indifference and inequalities that functional differentiation produces in practice (1997a: 776). Relatedly, Luhmann is of course aware that since functional differentiation is an evolutionary achievement, it makes no sense to see it as an unchangeable given. Functional differentiation is a contingent historical result and can be transcended and transformed by other modes of differentiation. Even more significant than the co-existence of forms of differentiation, Luhmann thus suggests that an entirely new mode of societal differen- tiation might materialise and replace functional differentiation in the future. It is this new mode of differentiation that I want to discuss in the following, and which Luhmann studies under the name inclusion/ exclusion.

Luhmann's analysis of inclusion and exclusion was briefly touched upon in Chapter 2 when examining his view on persons and individu- ality. As it was noted in that context, Luhmann argues that in the modern, functionally differentiated society individuality transforms into an exclusion individuality where the individual must create his or her individuality outside of the function systems. To recapitulate, inclusion refers to 'the way that humans are *indicated*, i.e. made relevant, in communication' (Luhmann 1995d: 241, italics in original). Luhmann speaks of exclusion when this is not the case. For example, a person is included in the economic system when he or she is addressed as a consumer. If the person is not addressed in the economic communication, he or she is excluded from the system. Luhmann insists that in modern society inclusion and exclusion are organised by function systems. It is the various function systems that decide when and how persons are addressed as relevant in the communication.

It is important to note that, contrary to what the concepts might suggest, exclusion is not per se bad, just as inclusion need not be attractive. As Armin Nassehi observes, 'an explicit insolvency is not an exclusion from the economic function system but a very specific form of *inclusion*, because *insolvency* is only possible if payments can be expected' (2002: 135, italics in original). Similarly, being punished in the legal system is a specific, but hardly desirable form of inclusion. Looking at the other side of the coin, temporary exclusion need not be problematic, just as exclusion from a single function system need not affect the individual negatively. For example, for some persons exclusion from art or religion can be completely unproblematic. However, as Rudolf Stichweh stresses, 'exclusion obviously becomes a problem if it happens repeatedly in the relations to plural social systems and if these exclusions are sequentially connected' (2002: 104).

Precisely the final part of this quote, the reference to the sequential connectedness of exclusions, is crucial, for it addresses the first of Luhmann's key assertions on the general dynamics of inclusion and exclusion in the modern, functionally differentiated society. Since, according to Luhmann, inclusion and exclusion are organised entirely by the various function systems, being included in one function system is no guarantee for inclusion in other function systems. Each function system is operationally closed and therefore applies its own specific criteria for inclusion and exclusion. This means, for example, that successful economic inclusion does not produce automatic scientific or political inclusion. This was discussed in Chapter 4 in terms of the strict separation of binary codes and the associated indifference of each system towards the operational logics of other systems. In the words of Luhmann, this decentralised organisation of inclusion amounts to a 'considerable *loosening of the integration* in the domain of inclusion' (1995d: 259, italics in original). Significantly, Luhmann adds, the exact opposite applies in the field of exclusion:

It is highly integrated because exclusion from one function system quasi automatically leads to exclusion from other function systems.

[…] An example from India: families that live on the street and do not have a permanent address cannot enrol their children in school.

(1995d: 259)

Another example: you lose your job and become excluded from the economic system. This means that you have no money to buy presents for the one you love. As a result of this and your complaints about having no job, he or she eventually kicks you out (exclusion from the system of love). You start to live on the street, and with no permanent address you do not receive your poll card, meaning that you become excluded from the political system. And so on. Although a bit exaggerated, the logic should be clear. One misfortune (exclusion) leads to the other, whereas one success (inclusion) need not lead to the next.

Importantly, for Luhmann, these are not mere theoretical reflections, derived from the abstract, conceptual logic of function systems. Quite the contrary, the strong integration of exclusion can be observed in many parts of the world. In an article entitled 'Beyond Barbarism', Luhmann describes the general state of affairs as he sees it, based on impressions collected first hand on his visits to these specific zones of marginalisation and exclusion. Let me quote at length:

exclusion still exists, and it exists on a massive scale and in such forms of misery that are beyond description. Anybody who dares a visit to the *favelas* of South American cities and escapes alive can talk about this. But even a visit to the settlements that were left behind after the closing of the coal mines in Wales can assure one of it. To this effect, no empirical research is needed. Who trusts his eyes can see it, and can see it so impressively that all explanations at hand will fail. We know: there is talk about exploitation, or about social suppression, or about *marginalidad*, about an increase of the contradiction between center and periphery. But all these are theories that are still governed by the desire for all-inclusion and therefore are looking for addressees to blame: capitalism, the ruling alliance of financial and industry capital with the armed forces or with the powerful families of the country. But if one takes a closer look, one does not find anything that could be exploited or suppressed. One finds existences reduced to the bodily in their self-perception and other-perception, attempting to get to the next day. In order to survive they have to have capabilities of perceiving dangers and of making available what is most needed – or resignation and indifference with regard to all "bourgeois" values: including order, cleanliness, and self-respect. And if one

adds up what one sees one can conceive of the idea that this may be
the guiding difference of the next century: inclusion and exclusion.
                    (Luhmann 2008a: 44–5, italics in original)

As the quote makes clear, what Luhmann is aiming at here is that usual
sociological accounts of marginalisation and exclusion do not hit the
target. When sociologists adhere to a classic vocabulary of exploitation
and seek to identify the alleged oppressors, they fail to see that the
contemporary exclusion patterns are now so far-reaching and penetrating that exploitation is actually an obsolete category. The problems
of today are much graver than any reference to exploitation allows us to
recognise, Luhmann believes.

Compared to Luhmann's other work, his discussion of inclusion and
exclusion stands out because of its emphatic – and, in a sense, politically
engaged – character. Contrary to scholars who favour an explicitly
critical-normative programme that attempts to change society for the
better, Luhmann typically assumes a cold attitude which seeks to register
and understand society, but which does not claim to be able to improve
it. In the analysis of inclusion and exclusion this is very different. To
be sure, Luhmann does not suddenly formulate a critical-normative
programme for political intervention. But the description of exclusion
dynamics in the favelas as well as his diagnosis/prognosis of inclusion/
exclusion as the new primary mode of societal differentiation is formulated in a clearly concerned voice. It is not that this mode of differentiation instigates a regression into a de-differentiated totalitarian regime, as
is often Luhmann's concern when he fears that functional differentiation
and its achievements are under pressure. Much more, the inclusion/
exclusion differentiation evokes an image of society which bears close
resemblances to a Hobbesian state of nature, hence reintroducing the
problem of social order (and double contingency).

As described in Chapter 4, Luhmann argues that the problem of social
order was solved historically by the development of symbolically generalised media of communication which sparked the emergence of codes
and function systems. Precisely these evolutionary achievements are
suspended in the favelas, Luhmann's analysis suggests. In ghettos and
favelas, there are no symbolically generalised media to handle double
contingencies. People are thrown on being constantly alert to the dangers
that lurk everywhere. As Friedrich Balke summarises Luhmann's analysis, '[i]n the zones of exclusion sociality, then, is more or less a question
of perception and not one of communication' (Balke 2002: 35). Indeed,
in Luhmann's account of the favelas, people are in effect reduced to sheer
bodies, focused entirely on basic bodily functions: 'they are running

about as bodies. [...] The most important questions are violence, sexuality and so on' (1994b: 5). In Balke's apt formulation, what Luhmann diagnoses here 'is in fact the *zero degree of social order*' (2002: 36, italics in original). It is a social order reduced to the most basic and fragile form possible. The complexities that characterise function systems are nowhere to be found in this zero–degree social order. Instead of an advanced functional differentiation, people are perceptually alert, always looking out for dangers and for ways to satisfy immediate bodily needs. Put differently, in the zones of exclusion that Luhmann describes, sociality is reduced to what Giorgio Agamben calls 'bare life', i.e. a life devoid of any value (Agamben 1998; Balke 2002: 27, 28).

Luhmann does not claim that inclusion/exclusion has already taken over as the new mode of societal differentiation. His analysis is more an account of important tendencies which, he believes, are lurking in some regions and will only be stronger in the years to come. This observation finds support in the work of other key sociologists, such as Zygmunt Bauman. According to Bauman, we are current living in a society which excludes people on a large scale and in a very systematic manner (e.g. 2002; 2004). Bauman speaks of wasted lives and observes the emergence of a new Big Brother logic to supplement the old one:

> The old Big Brother was preoccupied with *inclusion* – integrating, getting people into line and keeping them there. The new Big Brother's concern is *exclusion* – spotting the people who 'do not fit' into the place they are in, banishing them from that place and deporting them 'where they belong', or better still never allowing them to come anywhere near in the first place.
>
> (Bauman 2004: 132, italics in original)

Bauman claims that the work of the old and new Big Brothers goes hand in hand, although they operate in different zones. The new Big Brother fulfils his duties in the affluent parts of society, making sure that the wrong people do not get access, do not *get in*, to gated communities and societies. The old Big Brother operates in the traditional zones of exclusion, i.e. in ghettos, favelas, etc., and ensures that the people who live there do not cross the boundary and escape, do not *get out* (Bauman 2004: 132).

Luhmann's vocabulary differs. For him, it is not a matter of Big Brothers. Instead he speaks of a state 'beyond barbarism' (Luhmann 2008a). While the ancient Greeks distinguished between Hellenes and barbarians (in effect similar to the distinction between inclusion and exclusion), today it seems, so Luhmann's analysis suggests, that the zones of exclusion are beyond barbarism in the sense that they mark 'a space with no exit or escape' (Balke 2002: 30). In spite of this difference, Luhmann and Bauman share the insistence that modern society is increasingly being divided between those who are included and those who are not and who are therefore pulled into the zero-degree social order of perception and raw bodily tactics.

Luhmann's discussion of inclusion and exclusion triggers two important questions. First, is this a correct diagnosis at all? Second, what to do about the problem? Beginning with the former question it should be noted that Luhmann's proposition on weak integration on the side of inclusion and strong integration on the side of exclusion has provoked much debate. For example, Nils Mortensen (2004: 146) has argued that Bourdieu's (1986: 53–5) notion of conversion, which refers to the idea that one form of capital can be converted, at some cost, to other forms of capital, suggests that inclusion actually shows some form of integration across function systems. Moreover, Göbel and Schmidt (1998) have argued that Luhmann fails to convincingly substantiate the idea of the strong integration of exclusion.

For present purposes, I am more interested in assessing the validity of Luhmann's diagnosis on basis of a more methodological observation. For while Luhmann might seem to be acting out of character when it comes to his engaged attitude toward the inclusion/exclusion issue, this is even more pronounced when looking at the methodological approach he applies to capture this mode of differentiation. As explained in Chapter 3, Luhmann's sociological work from the late 1980s onward is characterised by an ever greater emphasis on second-order observation, observing how observing systems observe. Interestingly, this methodological approach is effectively suspended in Luhmann's analysis of inclusion and exclusion. More precisely, it is replaced with an ethnographic gesture, as Balke has convincingly demonstrated (Balke 2002). Thus, when Luhmann believes that the impressions he has acquired during his visits to the favelas are sufficient to account for what is going on there ('who trusts his eyes can see it'), this is certainly a first-order and not a second-order approach: Luhmann does not rely on how other observers observe, but is satisfied with his own immediate observations. As Balke puts it, referring to the famous anthropologist Clifford Geertz,

> Luhmann's texts on the zones of exclusion very clearly reveal the moment that their author, who is not very enthusiastic about empirical social research anyway, discovers his utter fascination with what Geertz calls the effect of "being there", that is, with fieldwork – though […] it is fieldwork in a rather unprofessional and somewhat touristic sense.
>
> (2002: 29)

One of the consequences of Luhmann's touristic and at any rate unsystematic fieldwork in the favelas is that his impressions are likely to foreclose that a new distinct form of sociality might have emerged here, which defies the logic of functional differentiation, but which also cannot simply be reduced to a play of mere bodily movements and adaptations. Precisely because Luhmann turns to first-order observations, he runs the risk that his own biases slip into his descriptions. And he ignores the possibility that the favelas are characterised by modes of sociality that he simply does not comprehend and which do not fit into his overall theoretical framework. It might be, for example, that functional equivalents to the symbolically generalised media of money, truth, art, etc. have emerged in the favelas, i.e. that new media have been developed which regulate double contingency in ordered ways, but in ways that are not be immediately comprehensible to an outside, first-order observer. My point is not that this is in fact the case; that a distinct form of sociality has indeed emerged in the favelas, which can neither be understood in terms of functional differentiation nor as a play between bodies. Rather, my critical point is that Luhmann's analysis is not open to this possibility. Luhmann considers himself able to make a valid account, based solely on his brief visits, and without taking alternative interpretations of what he experiences into consideration (see also Philippopoulos-Mihalopoulos 2008).

Even if one can problematise Luhmann's approach, this need not mean that his observations of the zones of exclusion are wrong. Nor need it imply that his diagnosis of the emerging mode of inclusion/exclusion differentiation is incorrect. This raises the question about what to do with these developments. Can they be reversed or impeded in any way, or do they assume an almost inevitable character? Luhmann surely does not put much faith in sociology as a discipline to direct a way out of the misery. 'If this diagnosis [of zones of exclusion, CB] is only roughly correct', he says, 'society can neither expect advice nor help from sociology' (2008a: 46). Moral concern and critical-normative blaming of, for example, capitalism would severely miss the target, Luhmann believes. Does this leave society in pure despair? Luhmann is not entirely pessimistic, but argues that the solutions must be found within the logics of functional differentiation. For example, he suggests that a new function system of social help might emerge, which is specialised in dealing with the effects of exclusion (1997a: 633). Alternatively, and more radically, he suggests that something be done which addresses the in a sense fundamental problem behind the exclusion dynamics he outlines, namely that function systems are characterised by *neglect* vis-à-vis one another. This neglect is a result of function systems being limited to the perspective of their particular binary code and medium. While this ensures specialisation, it also makes them unaware that the exclusion they produce may be amplified by other function systems (the strong integration on the exclusion side).[2] Against the background, Luhmann states that:

> It is very difficult to think of a political system which manages this kind of problems. The only possibility is actually to see how to introduce neglect into the neglecting system. That means how to make systems aware that they depend on indifference, on not looking at or not making an issue out of something, and how to make systems copy the difference of concern or unconcern into the system and then to see what can happen.
>
> (1994b: 5)

What Luhmann points at here is the need for *rationality* in the sense that function systems must learn to take into account how their communication affects the environment and how this might feed back onto the system. So, one could summarise Luhmann's position, in order to tackle the challenge that inclusion/exclusion might become the new primary mode of differentiation, it is crucial to stimulate function systems to take seriously how they relate to their environment.

Unfortunately, just as was the case in his discussion of ecological dangers, Luhmann offers no specific guidelines for how to accomplish this in practice. Yet he does stress, once again similarly to the ecological problematique, that this must be achieved through the various organisations that are related to the function systems (political organisations, corporations, etc.; see Luhmann 1994b: 5). Not only are organisations more dynamic and changeable than function systems; they can also span over several function systems at a time, and they are therefore more apt than function systems to take into account how exclusion from one system might lead to exclusion in other systems.

# 6

# Power and politics

Even if the de-centring of the modern, functionally differentiated society undermines the primacy often ascribed to politics, this obviously does not make the political system unimportant. The ability to make collectively binding decisions and to enforce them legitimately with physical force clearly are central capacities which call for sociological analysis. In this chapter I shall therefore go into more detail with Luhmann's conception of the political system. This will be executed in two steps. First, I will look into the internal differentiation of the political system that Luhmann describes. Next, I will explore his notion of politics in the welfare state. This includes a discussion of how Luhmann warns against certain trends in current political regulation which, he fears, lead to de-differentiation. Analysing these cautions will bring me back to the normative underpinnings of Luhmann's theory which are examined at length in this chapter.

Politics and power are closely related in Luhmann's theory. After the discussion of the political system, I therefore turn to his understanding of power. Here I first outline the kind of thinking on power that Luhmann finds obsolete or misleading. I then discuss his alternative conception of power, which, I claim, is based on two key pillars, namely the idea of power as a symbolically generalised medium of communication and the assertion that power is tied constitutively to the threat of activating negative sanctions. Having outlined these two pillars, I then examine how, according to Luhmann, power is exercised not politically, but in organisations. Finally, I return to the two pillars of Luhmann's theory of power. More specifically, I launch a critique of the negative sanctions pillar which, I contend, endows Luhmann's notion of power with an unfortunate, pre-modern bias.

In the discussions of power, I supply Luhmann's theory with input from Michel Foucault's analytics of power. The reason for drawing on Foucault in a discussion of Luhmann is that Foucault is widely recognised for his subtle historical analyses of power. Foucault's work may therefore serve as a critical contrast to the insights provided by systems theory. In particular, my critique of Luhmann's emphasis on negative sanctions is inspired by Foucauldian observations. Bringing together Luhmann and Foucault in a discussion of power should not gloss over the crucial differences between the two perspectives. However, in the present context, I am not interested in a fully-fledged comparison between Luhmann and Foucault. More modestly, I simply claim that a Foucauldian position can elucidate a particular weakness in Luhmann's conception of power, and that this can be seen as an invitation to improve Luhmann's work.

## THE INTERNAL DIFFERENTIATION OF THE POLITICAL SYSTEM

Chapter 4 described the political system as a societal subsystem whose function it is to make collectively binding decisions. The political system is not merely differentiated from other function systems but also contains its own internal differentiation. More specifically, Luhmann says, the system is organised around a 'threefold differentiation of *politics, administration* and *public*' (1990d: 47, italics in original). Here politics refers to the more narrow or genuine domain of politicians communicating about which collectively binding decisions are needed and how to make them. The administration denotes 'the totality of institutions that create binding decisions pursuant to political viewpoints and political mandate' (1990d: 48). This includes all sorts of administrative functions that operationalise and implement political decisions. Finally, the public refers to the audience of politics, and this is an audience that not only elects politicians once in a while but continuously affects them through polls, participation in the press, direct personal contact, etc. This threefold division at first sight parallels a traditional conception of the '"state organs" of parliament, government/administration and the electorate' (1990d: 49). In classical political science, the relation between these three organs is analysed as a basically hierarchical model: 'The parliament makes the laws and provides the means to get things done. The executive caries out the programs decided politically, while the public obeys the decisions and elects the parliament' (1990d: 49). Luhmann's analysis differs from this image in two important respects.

First, his preference for the notions of politics, administration and electorate (over those associated with 'state organs') signifies an attempt to loosen the understanding of the political system from a traditional state-biased conception. Indeed, he wishes to go beyond the tendency to equal the state and the political system. Against this image, he argues that 'the state' is nothing but the political system's self-description. That is, there is no such thing as the state in the sense of an organisational entity with imposing architecture and grand symbols, where one can knock on the door and voice one's concerns. Rather, the state is the *name* that the political system attributes to itself in modern society. So the state merely exists as a semantic reference, namely as something the political system can refer to to describe itself and increase its power:

> Interpreted as state authority, this power can legitimate itself as necessary [...]. Thus, the concept of the state can be used to charge politics with meaning and, at the same time, to limit its use. It [the state, CB] is more and also less than "mere politics".
>
> (1990e: 123)

In other words, the 'state' functions as a semantic pointer that at once endows the political system with importance (politics derives its legitimacy from the 'state') and puts limits to its reach (decisions cannot be made beyond 'the state's' powers; for example, UK politicians are not entitled to make decisions on Chinese infrastructure).

Second, the hierarchical model described above only designates the formal circuit of the political system's internal differentiation. In reality, Luhmann says, the moment this differentiation was effected, an informal 'counter cycle' emerged, which is still active today:

> The administration drafted the bills for politics and dominated parliamentary committees and similar institutions. Politics, with the help of its party organizations, suggested to the public what it should vote for and why. And the public exercised its influence on the administration through various channels, like interest groups and emotional appeals.
>
> (1990d: 49; see also 2000b: 253–65)

So rather than reducing the political system to a politics ➜ administration ➜ public model, Luhmann identifies a simultaneous and no less effective counter cycle where it is no longer clear what subsystem (politics, administration, public) is the more important one. As a result, the political system's internal differentiation is characterised by a de-centred structure, which to some extent resembles the de-centring of modern society that Luhmann's analysis of functional differentiation implies.

## POLITICS IN THE WELFARE STATE: EXPLICATING LUHMANN'S NORMATIVITY

While the internal differentiation between politics, administration and public describes how the political system is organised, it does not explain what, more specifically, the political system aims to ensure through its collectively binding decisions. Different political systems might have different overall goals but, according to Luhmann, the political systems that are usually called welfare states share one major objective. Thus, the aim of '[t]he welfare state is the realization of political inclusion' (1990d: 35). The political system of the welfare state simply seeks to attain that nobody is excluded from the political realm; that everyone is offered the means required to be part of the political system. (Recalling Luhmann's scepticism about the notion of the state, one might add that the welfare state is but the name with which a particular kind of political system, one aiming at political inclusion, describes itself).

More specifically, states Luhmann, the welfare state of today – and he is clearly speaking within a Northern-European context – is not merely concerned with the 'continuous improvement of the minimal standards of social well-being for everyone' (1990d: 36). Rather, ever new demands are raised which the welfare state is believed (by citizens and politicians alike) to be responsible for meeting so as to ensure political inclusion. More fundamentally, a veritable quest for compensation has emerged, he says, which forces the welfare state to compensate for all the 'disadvantages that befall the individual as a consequence of a particular way of living' (1990d: 22). This is the reason why 'safer docking facilities for Sunday sailors, hot-air dryers in public rest rooms etc.' (1990d: 36) are recognised as public goals, i.e. as something to be taken care of by the welfare state.

In order to offer this compensation and to satisfy all the claims that are directed at it, the welfare state in a sense transcends its political foundation and deploys the symbolically generalised media of law and money (1990d: 82). So even if these media are taken from non-political realms, they are so to speak appropriated by the political system to effectuate political goals. For example, if demands are raised for better education in public schools, the political system may allocate more money to text books, improved education of teachers and so on. Similarly, if demands are raised for safer roads, the political system can introduce new legal regulation that suggests tougher sanctions for traffic violations. Luhmann's point is that in either case, law and money enable the political system to say that something is actually done. 'We, the government, did listen to the concerns of the people and did therefore introduce new sanctions for traffic violation!'. Whether the measures, transformed into law and money, are effective or, on the contrary, produce perverse effects is a different matter – and, of course, something that can become a new political issue: 'We, the opposition, warned against the government's laxness and were right: no additional resources have been granted to the police, so the new sanctions for traffic violation are useless, for there is nobody to monitor if violations occur!'

Luhmann's main interest in the media deployed by the welfare state lies not so much in what can be achieved by them politically, but more in the structural limitations to their effectiveness that he identifies. To begin with, due to the operational closure of function systems, it is beyond the powers of the political system to determine what legal and economic effects the political use of law and money will have. This is regulated internally by the legal and economic systems. The reach of the political system is and remains restricted to ascertaining if the objectives on political inclusion are met. And this is, to repeat, an observation that follows a strictly political, rather than economic or legal, logic.

In addition to this, Luhmann stresses, while law and money 'provide external reasons for adjusting one's behaviour to specific conditions' (under the traditional assumption that if, for example, taxes are lowered, then people will work more), '[w]hat cannot be attained through law or money is the changing of people themselves' (1990d: 83–4, see also 92). Luhmann refers here to the attempts of the welfare state to correct or improve its citizens. Examples include therapeutic measures that seek to change the minds of criminals so that they will not make further offences, or attempts to endow unemployed people and other welfare recipients with an active ethos so that they seek means to support themselves of their own accord. According to Luhmann, this kind of 'people changing' or 'people processing' cannot be achieved through law and money. Indeed, he says,

> The principle of inclusion seems to find boundaries at the place where persons themselves have to be changed so that they can exploit the opportunities offered by society. Moreover, people changing is the most dangerous goal that politics can set itself. And even where adequate legitimation exists for the intrusion of "help," centralized technologies interested in responsibility and results are not available.
>
> (1990d: 84)

As the quote shows, Luhmann here oscillates between a factual and a normative position. Factually, he believes that the strict separation between social and psychic systems implies that there are clear limits to what can be attained by social means; there is simply no way of ensuring that the minds of people are reached and changed the way social systems might hope for. Normatively, Luhmann is very concerned about having people change as a political ideal. The underlying message he seems to convey is that such an endeavour amounts essentially to a totalitarian enterprise, where people are not allowed to have their own thoughts, but where these are subjected to political control. And yet, he complains, despite this potential totalitarian slide, the welfare state continues to regulate people through ever more money and law. This is problematic, Luhmann states, for the persistent recourse to money and law produces a fatal overload of these media. 'In the case of money, the welfare state costs too much. It promotes inflationary tendencies that in turn ruin it' (1990d: 84). In the case of law, ever new domains are subjected to legal regulation, meaning that aspects of people's lives which were previously left for people themselves to decide on (how to raise children, how to help the elderly, etc.) are now subjected to intense legal regulation. Luhmann is, of course, aware that the regulation effected by money and law always responds to specific problems that politicians and citizens perceive. But even if good reasons might be advanced in favour of this of that regulatory invention, the negative overload effects of it are usually ignored, he claims.

Interestingly, in his critical remarks on the overload of the media, Luhmann suddenly joins hands with Habermas who, in *The Theory of Communicative Action* (written around the same time as Luhmann published his analysis of the welfare state), famously warns against an increasing colonisation or rationalisation of the lifeworld through the media of money and power (Habermas 1984: 340–3). While Luhmann and Habermas converge in their critique of the expansion of the media of power, money and law, they do so on different normative grounds. Habermas advocates a left-wing position that places the respect for the lifeworld centrally. Luhmann, on his side, in effect champions a neo-liberal stance that focuses on setting limits to the political. I will say a few words on this interpretation of Luhmann as a neo-liberal theorist since it conflicts with Luhmann's self-proclaimed rejection of norma-tivity as well as with the doxa of systems theory where Luhmann's declared non-normativity is often taken for granted or accepted at face value.

To be sure, the assertion that Luhmann's theory promotes a liberal or conservative position is not new. This was a crucial part of the Frankfurt School's critique of Luhmann in the 1970s which argued that systems theory stimulated systemic conservation rather than societal change (see Chapter 1). As it happened, the gradual unpacking of Luhmann's political sociology in the 1980s and 1990s eventually proved the Frankfurt scholars right, although for the wrong reasons. Thus, it was not correct that Luhmann's sociology offered no platform from which to criticise modern society. Quite the opposite is the case. Throughout the 1980s and 1990s it becomes increasingly clear that Luhmann's notion of the operational closure of function systems serves not merely as a descriptive-analytical concept, but just as much as a normative lever for promoting an ideal of a minimal state. To discern this normative dimension of Luhmann's political writings, I will draw in the following on Chris Thornhill's brilliant analysis, to which I fully subscribe (Thornhill 2006).

Thornhill demonstrates how many of Luhmann's reflections on politics and the welfare state revolve around the question of *differentiation* and the lurking risks of *de-differentiation*. For example, Thornhill shows that, for Luhmann, the political system's legitimacy rests on it being differentiated from other function systems as well as the system being differentiated internally into politics, administration and public (Thornhill 2006: 40–1). Consequently, a potential de-differentiation of the political system vis-à-vis other systems or internally threatens its legitimacy. And such a de-differentiation does currently take place, Luhmann suggests, when – in the welfare state – the political system makes comprehensive use of law and money. Corresponding to the colonisation or rationalisation of the lifeworld that Habermas speaks of, Luhmann thus effectively identifies a *colonisation of systems* where, for example, legal regulation in the welfare state raises the question of 'whether the boundaries of what can be handled adequately by legal means are overstepped' (1990d: 85). Put differently, the welfare state's deployment of the medium of law at once questions the boundaries (i.e. the differentiation) not only between law and politics, but also between law and the fields that are now subjected to legal regulation (education, family life, etc.). Similarly, the welfare state constantly challenges the boundary between politics and economy because the political system's ample use of money tends to practically amalgamate the two systems (2000b: 216). In short, Luhmann argues, due to the welfare state's goal of political inclusion the political system is driven toward constant expansion, and this expansion or colonisation, which is buttressed by the deployment of law and money, destabilises the boundaries between the political system and the systems in its environment. Consequently, the welfare state actually, and paradoxically, threatens the strict differentiation that democracy relies on, and it therefore also threatens the legitimacy that is crucial to any modern political system.[1]

The notion of a colonisation of systems is mine, not Luhmann's, but it captures his concern and diagnosis. Moreover, it can be used to grasp a fundamental, but non-explicated tension in Luhmann's theorising on politics, 'steering' and de-differentiation. Thus, on the one hand, we learn that the political system in the welfare state transcends its boundaries, and in practice colonises other systems with de-differentiation effects. On the other hand, Luhmann is careful to emphasise that, actually, it is not possible at all for a system to surpass its boundaries. This is the whole gist of the theory of operationally closed systems. In an article entitled 'Limits of Steering' (1997b), Luhmann draws the full implications of this operational closure, arguing that no system can steer another system; the only kind of steering possible is self-steering. 'The political system is in this respect no exception; politics too can only steer itself, and if the steering refers to the environment then it is only to *its* environment' (1997b: 46, italics in original). While the steering of other systems is not possible, a system might create some irritation that affects another system, but this irritation is then filtered through the other system's self-steering. As indicated, this claim is founded theoretically on the idea of operationally closure, which implies that '[l]ike every system, *politics cannot transcend itself* and act on higher orders' (1997b: 47, italics· added). The tension becomes very clear here: on one hand, the operationally closed system of politics cannot operate outside its boundaries; on the other hand, this is precisely what it does in the welfare state, according to Luhmann. This might be interpreted as a tension between the theoretical apparatus and empirical-diagnostic observations. More significantly, however, I think it can be interpreted as an indication of Luhmann's normative problem with the welfare state: it is accused of something which, in other contexts, he finds impossible.

One of the alleged side effects of the expansionary character of the welfare state is, as mentioned above, its inflationary tendencies, economically as well as legally. It might be critically argued against this Luhmannian assertion that, even if money is a scare resource, it is not immediately clear why the welfare state should necessarily be approaching fiscal ruin (although its expenditures may indeed be problematised normatively-politically). This is but one example of how Luhmann fails to substantiate his attacks on the welfare state, hence contributing to the impression that his critique is politically motivated rather than (strictly) analytically grounded. Other examples of this include Luhmann's non-motivated claim that '[t]he possibilities of the welfare state seem have escaped' (2000b: 426); and his equally unsubstantiated emphasis on the 'foreseeable necessity to cut back the welfare state' (2000b: 428).

Still, his key concern remains centred on differentiation and de-differentiation. This concern is expressed as well in the recommendations he outlines for how to address the lurking problem of de-differentiation (and its negative implications for democracy). Significantly, Luhmann thus argues that '[a] reduction of politics to its function of satisfying the need for collectively binding decisions alone would fit better within the context provided by the functional differentiation of society' (1990d: 101). This quote intimates that the political system has indeed moved beyond its boundaries and that it is now time to withdraw to its proper function (making collectively binding decisions and nothing but that). Similarly, in the final chapter of his book on *Political Theory in the Welfare State* (a chapter which for some reason is not included in the English translation), Luhmann explicitly favours a 'restrictive understanding of politics' rather than an 'expansive' one (1981b: 156). Whereas the expansive model accepts ever more problems to fall under political regulation, the restrictive approach considers the 'limits to politics' and it even applies a functional method to show that there are alternatives to a *political* way of dealing with social problems (1981b: 156–7). So, in Luhmann's eyes, a proper understanding and re-structuring of the political system in the welfare state would have pull back the political system and demonstrate that there are functionally equivalent modes of addressing those issues that currently find political solutions.

It should be obvious from this discussion that, despite his claims to non-normativity and to presenting an apolitical sociological theory (see his comments on Habermas' critique in Luhmann 1971b: 398–405), Luhmann's analysis of the political system in the welfare state is penetrated by a clear normative-political programme. More specifically, as Thornhill aptly concludes,

> Luhmann attached himself more or less explicitly to a neo-liberal agenda in his account of the limits of state intervention and the dangers of de-differentiation. Indeed, throughout his theoretical career he endorsed the restriction of the number of themes (especially economic and educational) which are deemed susceptible to politicization and so supported a model of the minimal state and a minimal conception of politics.
>
> (Thornhill 2006: 50, n. 8)

Let me stress finally that the analysis of Luhmann's normativity only concerns his reflections on politics and the political system and how they relate to an underlying question of differentiation versus de-differentiation. I do not contend that his sociological theory as such has a normative bias, and also do not think that such a claim could be substantiated. Thus, there is no inherent normative message in the separation between system and environment, just as his focus on how systems operate does not induce a specific, for example, conservative horizon.

After this examination of the normative underpinnings of Luhmann's theory of politics in the welfare state I will now turn to a discussion of his notion of power. For although the political system in the welfare system makes widespread use of law and money, these media are deployed, essentially, as means to exercise power.

## LUHMANN ON POWER: BEYOND CLASSICAL THEORIES

It was noted in Chapter 4 that, for Luhmann, power is one of several symbolically generalised media of communication, more specifically a medium that serves to ensure that ego makes alter's action a premise for his or her own action (the Aa ➔ Ea scheme). To see the full ramifications of this notion of power, it is crucial to understand the kind of framework it responds to and seeks to correct and go beyond.[2] In particular, Luhmann aims to transcend what he calls 'classical theory of power', as it appears in political science and sociology. Before exploring how Luhmann wrestles with this classical theory it should be noted that his main publications on the topic were published in the years between 1969 and 1975. So it is the kind of theorising that was prominent at this time that he engages with, and not the subsequent inventive contributions to the understanding of power that for instance Michel Foucault has put forward. Let me also note that when Luhmann speaks of 'classical theory of power', he is no doubt painting with a broad brush, underplaying the internal varieties that may characterise the positions which are lumped together under this umbrella category. Similar to Luhmann, however, I will not problematise this categorisation.

According to Luhmann, the classical theory of power is epitomised in Herbert A. Simon's definition of power. Simon famously argues that, 'for the assertion, "A has power over B", we can substitute the assertion, "A's behavior causes B's behavior"' (quoted in Luhmann 1969: 150, n. 3). Luhmann believes that this conception of power is misleading on several accounts. Most importantly, it analyses power in terms of causality and assumes that power is what causes the subordinate to behave in a specific way and that this behaviour would not have occurred, had there been no exercise of power. Luhmann is very critical of causal explanations since, he believes, causality is never something that exists 'out there'; rather, it is an attribution made by an observer, and this observer could have pointed to other effects of the same cause, or to other causes behind a given effect (this is his basic reason for turning the interest from causality to the functional method).

A further problem with the classical understanding of power is that it posits power as some kind of substance that the power-holder possesses

(Luhmann 1969: 158–9). This is misleading, Luhmann says, because it assumes that power is a thing that, like an object, can be possessed, kept away, reintroduced, transferred to somebody else, etc. By seeing power as a substance to be possessed, the systemic conditions that make the exercise of power possible are easily ignored. This image of power as a possession also easily implies that, to study power, one should look for the persons who are believed to 'hold' power at a specific moment. In other words, the possession approach easily gives way to an individual-istic account where power is attributed to individuals. Finally, the notion of power as a possession conjectures that power is a zero-sum game where more power on one side must necessarily lead to less power for someone else. According to Luhmann, this is a questionable assump-tion (see Luhmann 1969: 163; 1979: 179–82). I will come back to this below when discussing power in organisations.

Interestingly, Foucault's attempt to develop a contemporary under-standing of power also surpasses the premises of classical theories of power. As Foucault sees it, what needs to be overcome is what he calls the discourse of sovereignty or the juridico-political image of power. This image is based on three key assumptions (see Foucault 1990: 94–6; Lemke 1997: 99). First, it assumes that power is a substance that can be *possessed*, exchanged, etc., which implies that power is seen as a zero-sum game. Second, this image of power presumes that power is *located* a specific place, typically in a centre or a 'headquarter' (the monarch, the state, etc.) from which it then flows to the rest of society. Finally, the sovereign image of power contends that power serves to *repress*, meaning that, according to this notion, power and freedom constitute one anoth-er's opposites: when power is exercised, repression rules and freedom is suspended. Foucault describes how this notion of power emerged in a specific historical context:

> Through the development of the monarchy and its institutions this juridico-political dimension was established. It is by no means adequate to describe the manner in which power was and is exer-cised, but it is the code according to which power presents itself and prescribes that we conceive of it. The history of the monarchy went hand in hand with the covering up of the facts and procedures of power by the juridico-political discourse.
>
> (Foucault 1990: 87–8)

This historisation indicates the analytical point that Foucault is aiming at. The juridico-political image of power corresponds to a particular social structure which is long superseded. But even if this image of power is outdated, the juridico-political conception of power nevertheless retains its hold in contemporary social and political theory. In an often-quoted remark, Foucault therefore complains that 'we still have not cut off the head of the king' (1990: 88–9). In other words, contemporary understandings of power still assume that power is something that is possessed at a centre and used to repress others. Against this background, Foucault's ambition is to demonstrate that and how power is exercised in more subtle forms that defy this image.

This is not the place to examine Foucault's complex genealogy of power. Suffice it say that in *Discipline and Punish* (1977), he develops a notion of power as discipline, which emphasises the positive and productive aspects of power as opposed to the negative–repressive ones which are stressed by the discourse of sovereignty. In some of his later work, he identifies a concern with power in the form of government, defined as 'conduct of conduct', or action upon action. Conceived as government, to exercise power is 'to structure the possible field of action of others', or of oneself (1982: 221). This notion of power, which is derived from Foucault's study of liberalism, counters the idea that power is opposed to freedom. Thus, Foucault states, '[p]ower is exercised over free subjects, and only insofar as they are free' (1982: 221). Similarly, this notion of power does not assume an underlying causal model, nor that power is possessed by someone located in a headquarter (see also 1990: 94–5).

It should be clear from this that Foucault shares certain starting points with Luhmann. Specifically, the two scholars are surprisingly close to one another when it comes to identifying the classical assumptions that need to be overcome. They go in different directions, however, when formulating their alternative conceptions of power. Whereas Luhmann proposes a sociological theory of power, Foucault deliberately abstains from a sociological framework. His aim is not to develop a theory of power, but rather to investigate historically how power is conceptualised and problematised in different epochs. I shall come back to Foucault on more occasions in the following when discussing the main elements of Luhmann's sociological theory of power.

## THE TWO PILLARS OF POWER

How does Luhmann surpass the misleading assumptions of classical theories of power? What does his alternative notion of power look like? I will argue that Luhmann's theory of power is constituted by two central pillars, both of which reveal ample inspiration from Parsons. The first pillar is the functional or medial notion of power. The second pillar suggests that power is constituted by negative sanctions. The first pillar was already introduced in Chapter 4 in the discussion of double contingency and the symbolically generalised media of communication and need not be repeated here. Suffice to recall that, according to this view, the function of the medium of power is to render probable that ego uses alter's action as a premise for his or her own action, or, differently put, the medium of power serves to motivate ego to condition his or her action by alter's action (Luhmann 1997a: 355; 2000b: 60).

Interestingly, this conception of power as a relation between action and action is structurally equivalent to Foucault's definition of government as conduct of conduct – with the twist that Luhmann's theory of symbolically generalised media of communication is explicitly concerned with the regulation of *selections*, of selected action upon selected action (1976: 517). The medial conception of power also displays a resemblance to Foucault's emphasis on the intimate relation between power and freedom. In Luhmann's theory, this is implied by the concept of selection. If ego *cannot* act in opposition to alter's request, then there is no need for power at all. Coercion marks the end of power. As a result, coercion always comes at a certain cost: 'The person exercising coercion must himself take over the burden of selection and decision to the same degree as coercion is being exercised [...] the reduction of complexity is not distributed but is transferred to the person using coercion' (1979: 112). To illustrate, if an employee coerces an employee to do a specific task, then the employer alone has the responsibility should anything unexpected occur. It might be, for instance, that the specific assignment was illegal. In that case, the employee can excuse him or herself by saying that he or she was coerced into doing the offence (he or she had *no choice*), and so the employer assumes full responsibility.

Luhmann's theory of symbolically generalised media of communication is inspired in part by Parsons' work. The Parsonian legacy is even more pronounced in the second pillar of Luhmann's theory of power. Similarly to Parsons (1969), Luhmann thus establishes a constitutive link between power and negative sanctions. Power simply depends on the possibility of activating negative sanctions, Luhmann claims. He states, for instance, that 'the concept of *negative sanction* is indispensable' to characterise power as a symbolically generalised medium of communication (1990f: 157, italics in original). Elsewhere he contends that '[p]olitical power is essentially a threatening power. At any rate, one cannot conceive of it without this component' (1988a: 45).

It is important to note that the reference to sanctions does not mean that power is realised through the actual use of sanctions. Rather, the sanction refers to an alternative or an option, which ego as well as alter would prefer to avoid (a so-called 'avoidable alternative'), but which it may be necessary for alter to fall back on in case ego does not use alter's action as a premise for his or her own action. Obviously, the sanction is directly unpleasant to ego who is hit by it. But alter, too, would prefer to avoid the sanction, for its realisation means that the mere threat was insufficient to generate the preferred actions of ego. For example, coercion might be required, and that marks, as mentioned above, the end of power. So power is only exercised as long as the negative sanctions remain a possibility, an option not yet realised. Importantly, moreover, even if both ego and alter would prefer to avoid the sanction, the two parties have a very different appraisal of its realisation. Thus, the power-holder (alter) can better live with the sanction than the power-subject (ego) can. For example, if an employer (alter) bases his or her power on the threat of firing the employee (ego), then realising this sanction will be annoying to the employer (who will have to find someone else to do the work or, even worse, do it him or herself), but in the end it is the employee who must bear the brunt since he or she is the one losing the job. It is precisely this difference that constitutes the power of the powerful, Luhmann says: alter is simply less averse to the actual use of sanctions than ego is. Luhmann also expresses this in a Spencer-Brown-inspired manner when stating that the two-sided form of power is execution of the order⌐ execution of the sanction (see Luhmann 1997a: 356).

The emphasis on how power, and hence also political power, relies on negative sanctions may come as a surprise, given the previous discussion of how the political system in the welfare state ensures political inclusion by granting ever more money. How does this positive gesture fit to the image of negative sanctions? To be sure, Luhmann says, the welfare state does indeed apply 'positive sanctions' when it offers social benefits of different sorts and compensates for this or that disadvantage. At the same time, he claims, a '*law of the transformation of positive sanctions into negative ones*' applies: 'If assistance occurs with a certain regularity, if services are expected, if the contributions of others to one's own living are customary, then their loss becomes a threat, their withdrawal a possible sanction' (1990f: 158, 159, italics in original). In other words, the welfare state exercises power by keeping open the possibility of withdrawing benefits or services, i.e. of transforming positive sanctions into negative sanctions.

Two final points are warranted. First, as should already be clear, Luhmann leaves open what kinds of sanctions the exercise of power rests on. The ultimate negative sanction is physical violence, but its legitimate use remains limited. Hence more subtle alternatives have emerged, such as transforming positive sanctions into negative ones. Since negative sanctions may assume many diverse forms, empirical sociological work is needed to examine what sanctions are at stake and how they function in the exercise of power.

Second, Luhmann argues that 'the concept of symbolic generalisation makes it possible to transfer the concepts of *deflation* and *inflation* from the theory of money into the theory of power' (1990f: 164, italics in original). For example, empty threats produce an inflation of power. If alter fails to actualise the negative sanctions in case of non-compliance, then power loses its power, so to speak. By contrast, power is deflated if the power-holder does not make sufficient use of the power that is attributed to him or her. This would happen, for instance, if on too many occasions an employer fails to demand that his or her employees regulate their action according to what he or she determines, thereby failing to demonstrate and reproduce the power structure (1979: 165–6).

## POWER IN ORGANISATIONS

According to Luhmann, the political system provides a systematic reproduction of political power. Yet power may also be identified outside of the political system, although here power will often be exercised on a more 'parasitic' basis, since in families, in the economy, in science, etc. there are no systemic structures to back up a continuous reproduction of power (2000b: 69). Of course, power hierarchies can be detected in, for example, science where professors are often more powerful than students. But this is not due to scientific communication, Luhmann would argue, for there is nothing in the scientific code true/false that could create an enduring reproduction of power. Rather, it is an effect of the particular *organisation* of universities that modern science in structured around. It therefore makes sense to look into how power is exercised in contemporary organisations, since in modern society, non-political power is typically exercised continuously 'on the basis of formal organization' (1990f: 160). Formal organisations refer, as noted in Chapter 4, to social systems that have rules for membership and operate through decision making.

Luhmann distinguishes between two main forms of power in organisations (1979: 177–9). The first, 'organisational power', works by using the potential to exclude people as its negative sanction. If the employee does not execute the orders, then he or she may lose his or her membership of the organisation, typically by being fired. The problem with this form of power is that it is not very flexible. It would be highly unpractical if people were dismissed every time they refused to obey orders: the more specialised an organisation is, the more knowledge the individual employees gather which they alone possess and which it is difficult to replace through new-hires. This means that the alternative to be avoided (the sanction) becomes increasingly costly to the organisation. The organisation is therefore interested in pursuing other forms of power that regulate the employees' actions, but do so in a way where 'organisational power' is only the very last resort. Consequently, Luhmann states, organisations exercise so-called 'personnel power', which focuses on which positions in the organisation people may achieve and possibly lose. More specifically, this form of power regulates the action of the employees by threatening to place the latter in less attractive positions within the organisation. In other words, this form of power conditions action through career sanctions. The play between positive and negative sanctions that Luhmann analyses in the case of the welfare state therefore also applies to how power is exercised in organisations:

> Organizational power is ultimately nothing more than a case of the application of the transformation of positive sanctions into negative ones. It rests on the fact that membership in organizations and especially the occupation of higher positions can be bestowed as an *advantage*, and its non-bestowal or withdrawal can be affixed as a *negative sanction*.
>
> (1990f: 162, italics in original)

One of the specific features of organisations is that they allow very easily for a particular extension of power. In Luhmann's general conception of power as a symbolically generalised medium of communication power regulates the double contingency of alter and ego. While this is the primeval situation of sociality, the social at its minimal form, it does not account for situations of more than two parties. But power may also regulate the action of more than one ego. This is what happens in so-called 'chains of action' where A exercises power over B who exercises power over C who exercises power over D, etc. (1979: 132–4). Luhmann emphasises that a chain of action does not refer to some diffuse influence. The chain only exists insofar as A has disposal over B's *power* over C, etc. As Luhmann explains, a chain does not exist simply:

> if the king can command the general, if the latter can give his wife orders and she her servants likewise, who, because of their position, can tyrannize their neighbours. [...] a chain only exists if and in so far as the power-holder can intervene in the chain.
>
> (1979: 133)

Chains of action enable a kind of government or 'action at a distance', as Nikolas Rose has put it in his Foucault-inspired work (1996: 43). They endow alter with the capacity to exercise power throughout the organisation. The boss need not tell each employee individually what he or she should do (in a large organisation this would be practically impossible), but can delegate this task to managers and middle managers. 'Chain formation thus makes possible increases in power which go beyond the selection capacity of the individual power-holder' (1979: 133–4).

At the same time, these chains effect a counter cycle similar to the one Luhmann observes with respect to the relation between politics, administration and the public within the political system. This has two dimensions. First, for every link added to the chain, more possibilities emerge for the individual nodes to use the power that the chain endows them with for their own purposes (1979: 133). The longer the chain is, the more difficult it becomes to control such local 'parasites'. Relatedly, second, an ever greater information asymmetry is likely to occur as new links are added to the chain. The power 'centre' (A) simply does not have access to all the information and knowledge that is produced locally. In combination, these two dimensions imply that chains of action will not only increase the power of the 'centre' (A), but just as much of each link in the chain (B, C, D, etc.). In fact, states Luhmann, when the complexity of organisations increases, this will be to the advantage of the employees, as they will become more powerful due to insertion of the chains of action that the complexity demands. More generally, this demonstrates that chains of action effect a plus–sum game of power rather than a zero–sum game, thereby undermining one of the central implications of classical theory of power.

To be sure, this play between formal chains of power and their informational counter cycles may not be visible to outside observers. 'Viewed from outside, the homogeneity of the organisation and the ability to implement organisational power is typically overestimated. Power is attributed to the top, while in truth complicated balances of power exist that vary, especially with topics and situations' (1990f: 163). Interestingly, Luhmann claims, even if such external descriptions of the organisation are far from adequate, they nevertheless can produce significant internal effects and give rise to new informal power positions. Most importantly, the organisation's top can utilise the external image of it in internal power struggles:

> Top level persons can threaten to leave the organization or otherwise create situations that make it apparent to the environment that the organization does not function like a decisional and implementational unity. This forms the basis of a kind of informal power of the formal top that rests merely on the fact that power is attributed to it and this attribution [...] is sensitive to information about facts.
> (1990f: 164)

To summarise the discussion so far, Luhmann operates with a double-pillar conception of power where power is seen both as a medium and as constitutively tied to negative sanctions. And this notion of power is applied both to the realm of political power, centred around and reproduced by the political system, and to the exercise of power that takes place outside of the political system, most notably in organisations.

## GETTING RID OF SANCTIONS: A CRITIQUE

I would like to end the discussion of power by inquiring into how evident the link between power and negative sanctions is. More specifically, I believe that the assertion that power relies on negative sanctions represents what I would call a semantic short-circuit in Luhmann's theory. To see this, it is important to go back to Foucault's analytics of power. Bearing Foucault's work in mind, it thus appears as if Luhmann reinstalls one of the central characteristics of the juridico-political image of power, namely its negativity (the repression dimension, the reliance on threats). As Foucault shows, this negative image of power corresponds to a specific pre-modern social order: a hierarchically differentiated society with a monarch at the top who exercises his or her power by repressing the subordinates. Although Luhmann would reject that power can be possessed (by a monarch or others) and that it be located a specific place in society (e.g. in the feudal top), his insistence on linking power to negative sanctions in effect means that his notion of power is embedded in an 'Old-European' or outdated semantics where power relies on the possibility of sanctioning non-compliance. The notion of 'Old-European semantics' is Luhmann's. He usually employs this notion to refer to pre-modern semantics that reappear in modern society, but which is no longer adequate since the societal structure, to which the vocabulary initially corresponded, has been replaced by functional differentiation.

As Foucault is careful to note, the negative conception of power is not necessarily wrong. Obviously, even today much power is based on the ability to sanction non-compliance. For example, the action of employees might be regulated by the threat of firing them. However, this negative image is nevertheless highly inadequate to account for the forms of power that are exercised today, and which, so Foucault argues, should rather be analysed in terms discipline, government, etc. Indeed, the whole idea of these forms of power is that they represent *positive* rather than negative modes of regulating action. For example, they seek to modulate subjects in such a way that they act as desired *by their own accord*, i.e. without having sanctions in reserve in case of non-compliance. For example, the management of contemporary knowledge workers need not rely on the threat of negative sanctions. Instead, power is exercised over these knowledge workers by installing in them an ethos which prescribes constant work. That is, the power operates by infusing the workers with a desire to work 24/7.

Returning to Luhmann, I will argue that, given the discussion above, the negative sanctions pillar of his theory of power runs counter to his own objectives in a double sense. On the one hand, it is at odds with his theory of functional differentiation because the constitutive notion of sanctions suggests that his conception of power corresponds to a pre-modern hierarchically differentiated society. On the other hand, the constitutive tie between power and negative sanctions a priori forecloses the possibility that power could be exercised in ways that differ from what the Old-European semantics implies. By deducing the actual operations of power from the prevailing (pre-modern) semantics of power, as Luhmann tends to do, one runs the risk of ignoring historical transformations in the exercise of power.

How, then, to handle this critique? Does it mean that Luhmann's theory of power collapses? I think not. Yet I do believe that some adjustment is warranted. Specifically, I would argue for loosening the relation between power and negative sanctions, and seeing the latter as just one of many ways of conditioning action through action. While downplaying the negative sanctions pillar, the functional understanding of power (as an evolutionary result of the need for regulating the contingencies of alter's and ego's actions) could be emphasised instead. Highlighting only this functional pillar would have two important advantages. First, Luhmann's theory of power would acquire a more open and empirically sensitive form, where it would be an empirical question how and by what means alter's action functions as a premise for ego's action. Second, and this would be a key addition as compared to a Foucauldian perspective, the functional approach to power would be consistent with Luhmann's emphasis on functional differentiation. That is, focusing merely on the functional pillar retains the Luhmannian interest in analysing power sociologically, including how it relates to various forms of societal differentiation.

Elsewhere I have utilised this emphasis on the functional-medial pillar to demonstrate how the formation of subjectivities, which constitutes a key interest in Foucault's analytics of power, can be incorporated into Luhmann's systems theory, namely as a form of so-called 'semantic intrusion' (see Borch 2005b: 162–4). This is but one example of how Luhmann's sociology of power would acquire a greater sensitivity to empirical variations in the exercise of power if the focus on negative sanctions were downplayed.

# 7

# Conclusion

It has only been possible to sketch and discuss a fraction of Luhmann's impressive sociological work in this book. I have tried to draw attention to a number of the central concepts in his systems theory, just as I have attempted to convey a sense of how Luhmann approaches and studies social phenomena. While this cannot conceal the fact that there are many layers of his work that have not been addressed here, I do hope to have indicated some of the main conceptual and analytical contributions of Luhmann, which might prove helpful in future sociological studies. In this final chapter I would like to summarise what I conceive as the chief sociological achievements of Luhmann, to point to some blind spots in his work and, at the end, to suggest what it might mean to follow in the footsteps of Luhmann.

## LUHMANN'S MAIN SOCIOLOGICAL ACCOMPLISHMENTS

There are different ways to assess a sociological theory. In Luhmann's case, it makes sense to discuss his sociological importance, both with respect to each of the three phases of his work and in terms of the more general achievements that go across the three phases.

Each of the three phases offers important sociological contributions. In the first phase, which in many ways is the least radical one, Luhmann's key sociological contribution lies in his formulation of a functionalist programme that goes beyond the Parsonian legacy. By emphasising the functionalist–structuralist approach as an alternative to Parsons' structural functionalism, Luhmann suggests a new way of conceiving what functionalism may look like today. (It might be argued that Luhmann was not entirely successful in this move, as many commentators continued to associate him with Parsons' work). This Luhmannian functionalism, which as described in Chapter 1 is a comparative approach to the study of possible relations between problems and solutions, is a valuable tool that not only enters his notion of a sociological enlightenment, but points to a broader field of applicability. Thus, I contend, Luhmann's comparative functionalism is an important analytical instrument that can be employed to demonstrate the contingency of the social world. Whatever is seen as natural or necessary can be functionally deconstructed, as it were, showing that what is currently observed as an obvious relation between a given problem and a given solution could be conceived differently. For example, in an organisation it may become second nature for managers to deal with recruitment challenges in a specific way (posting available positions in particular newspapers). Here the functionalist method provides a tool of reflection for conceiving problem and solution in a fresh light. In short, therefore, by emphasising this comparative functionalism, Luhmann invites sociologists and non-sociologists alike to think differently and to go beyond what is held as true and right at any given moment: could we think of new solutions, and could a reflection on current solutions lead to a new perspective on problems? Obviously, Luhmann is not the only sociologist and social theorist who takes contingency seriously. Foucault is another scholar who continuously demonstrated that knowledge and subjectivities must be seen as historical phenomena, and hence as changeable, contingent ones. Yet what is distinctive about Luhmann's approach is that this concern with contingency is embedded in a strict sociological methodology, and that this methodology is placed centrally in his work.

The main sociological contribution of the second phase of Luhmann's work is clearly his conception of the social as consisting of autopoietic systems of communication. This has two sides, one being the understanding of sociality as a matter of communication; the other being the assertion that communication (social systems) is organised autopoietically. In both respects Luhmann's theoretical innovations must be credited as formidable achievements. By seeing the social as communication Luhmann not merely subscribes to the linguistic turn of social theory, which places language and communication centrally for the conception of social life. Much more, Luhmann actually draws the most radical implications of this linguistic turn when he argues that society and the social are nothing but communication and that only communication communicates. No other sociologist provides such a radical, and still conceptually consistent, view on the self-constitution of society. The associated autopoietic understanding of communication is no less of an accomplishment. Indeed, the examination of the sociological consequences of autopoiesis (most notably, the emphasis that social systems cannot transcend their boundaries) constitutes one of Luhmann's central contributions to social theory. The autopoietic scaffold not only bears witness to an impressive theoretical inventiveness; it also provides a theoretical substantiation of the idea of the communicative self-constitution of society.

While the functionalist approach is methodological in character, the communicative-autopoietic framework serves a more theoretical-analytical function. It describes the constitution and fundamental operational mode of the social, and this provides the platform for conducting empirical research of specific social systems, their operational logics and interrelations.

Finally, in the third phase of this work, Luhmann's key contribution to sociology lies in his emphasis on second-order observation. While this turn is related to Luhmann's increasing interest in epistemological issues, it also carries more mundane sociological implications. Most importantly, the theory of second-order observation in effect installs a methodological programme that invites the sociologist to change the centre of attention from 'what' questions to 'how' questions. So rather than describing *what* the social world looks like (e.g. on basis of statistics), Luhmann asks the sociologist to describe the social through observations of *how* observers observe it. More specifically, this methodological programme asks 'who is the observer observing, and how, i.e. on basis of what distinctions, does the observer observe?'

When looking at the more general accomplishments of Luhmann, those transcending the three phases (or at least going beyond more of them), especially five contributions should be highlighted. First of all, Luhmann has placed theory centrally on the sociological agenda. Rather than gathering new amounts of empirical data, his passion for theory has led him to insist on the need for a new theoretical edifice for sociology. Relatedly, he has argued that the theoretical crisis he identifies in previous sociology can only be redeemed through a new grand theory of society. One might not share the view that such a grand theory is needed, let alone possible to formulate, but Luhmann nevertheless deserves credit for attempting to establish such a grand theory – and even more so for actually succeeding with it. This has been achieved through an impressive theoretical inventiveness, which has taken as its starting point the apparently innocent distinction between system and environment. Luhmann's second general contribution consists in the constant elaboration of what this system/environment distinction entails. Third, Luhmann's theory of functional differentiation is a central update of classical sociological debates on modern society's structuring traits. Here Luhmann has offered a penetrating analysis of (the evolution of) operationally distinct societal domains, just as he has cautioned against too easy diagnoses of new societal transformations (postmodernity, late modernity, etc.). Relatedly, he has emphasised the achievements of functional differentiation, not least with respect to democracy, and has thereby provided a passionate defence of modernity.

While these three contributions have all received ample attention throughout the present book, the final two contributions that I will highlight have been discussed only more cursory. Thus, fourth, Luhmann has accomplished the formulation of a comprehensive sociology that does not revolve around the human subject. This was a key consequence of the understanding of social systems as systems of communication. By abandoning the humanist tradition Luhmann has sided with poststructuralist scholars from other fields, and his main contribution here can be seen as representing a strong *sociological* (and not primarily philosophical) voice in the poststructuralist landscape. Fifth, and finally, Luhmann has taken time seriously in all of his work. This dates back to an early interest in combining sociological theory with evolutionary objectives. Yet this interest in understanding the temporal aspects of sociality is also visible in many subsequent discussions, from the inclusion of time as one of the three meaning dimensions, over analyses of how functional differentiation entails a differentiation of temporal horizons to discussions on temporal aspects of specific function systems (notably, law and economics).

## BLIND SPOTS IN LUHMANN'S THEORY

As Luhmann emphasises in his discussions of first and second-order observation, every observation contains a blind spot. This obviously also applies to Luhmann's own observations. By choosing system/environment as the guiding analytical distinction, Luhmann is blinded toward aspects of social life that cannot easily be captured through this distinction. More specifically, the particular ways that Luhmann employs and interprets the system/environment distinction produces blind spots in his analytical gaze. In the following I will pinpoint some of the flaws or blind spots in Luhmann's sociology.

The first blind spot is *space* (see also Filippov 2000). I have already discussed Luhmann's lack of systematic attention to spatiality in previous chapters, summarised most notably in his statement that social systems 'are not at all spatially limited, but have a completely different, namely purely internal form of boundary' (1997a: 76). According to Luhmann, the distinction between system and environment is simply not spatial in any way. To be sure, in some instances Luhmann does recognise the importance of space. This applies to his understanding of interaction systems which, through their dependence on co-presence and reflexive perception, are bound to specific spaces. Similarly, in *Art as a Social System* Luhmann offers a discussion of space, although mainly in terms of how it appears as a 'neurophysiologic operation of the brain' (Luhmann 2000a: 111). Finally, his exploration of zones of exclusion in effect demonstrates that 'under certain circumstances environments turn out to be spatial' (Balke 2002: 30). Yet the spatial character of these spatial environments is not systematically analysed by Luhmann.

Luhmann's 'de-privileging of the spatial dimension' (Stichweh 1998: 343) is surprising for several reasons. First of all, it seems as if this de-privileging is the result of an active theoretical choice, rather than a coincidental outcome. For example, Maturana's understanding of autopoietic systems contains an explicit reference to spatiality (see Chapter 2), but this spatial dimension does not survive Luhmann's adoption of the concept of autopoiesis. But the lack of attention to spatiality is also surprising for analytical reasons. As geographers and spatial theorists have demonstrated, specific spatial settings make some communications more likely than others, meaning that space may have crucial implications for social systems. For example, some buildings and rooms inspire creativity, whereas others do the opposite. In Luhmann's vocabulary, this might be conceived as a structural coupling between spatiality and sociality. In fact, this is how Rudolf Stichweh seeks to remedy this Luhmannian blind spot. According to Stichweh, we should see space as a structural coupling to society, a suggestion which, he admits, would interfere with the 'Luhmannian *dogma* that society is only structurally coupled to consciousness' (Stichweh 1998: 348, italics in original).

The next blind spot I will call attention to concerns social systems' operational level and ontological status. Although Luhmann would strongly reject that his systems theory contains any ontology at all, I believe it is warranted to argue that his understanding of autopoietic systems unwittingly installs a specific ontology, namely what I would call an *operations ontology* according to which there can only be one type of operations per system. Social systems are characterised by communication only; the legal subsystem by legal operations only; the economic system by economic operations only, etc. This makes sense from a theoretical point of view, in that it follows from Luhmann's conception of autopoietic self-reproduction. However, the one system–one operation assertion also produces a particular blind spot, namely an inattentiveness to the possibility that, empirically, function systems might exist or emerge that reproduce themselves through several types of operations.

Luhmann's conception a priori forecloses this possibility and thus produces a lack of empirical sensitivity. For example, what Luhmann might analyse in terms of code clashes between an economic and a scientific code might more aptly be examined as the emergence of a new type of system which is organised around a double economic and scientific mode of operation.

The third blind spot concerns the *relations* between system and environment. Despite suggesting notions such as structural coupling and interpenetration it is hard to escape the impression that Luhmann's theory has only little to offer when it comes to understanding how systems relate to their environment, including system/system relations. While systems theory proposes a sophisticated account of internal systemic processes, the description of relations to the systems' outside remains a rather weak and underdeveloped side. Both as a theoretical concept and in the specific empirical analyses that Luhmann (and others) have put forward, structural coupling often tends to work as a 'magic' concept. Relations always end up being structural couplings. But how much is actually said, one might critically ask, when it is asserted that systems are structurally coupled? Would it not be more interesting to show in detail how the couplings emerge, develop, are maintained, etc. and what specific implications they have. Relatedly, are couplings to be analysed in a binary manner (either they exist or they don't), or could it be that they are subject to degrees in intensity, so that some couplings are stronger than other? Such questions remain largely unexplored within Luhmann's theory. These critical reflections are not meant to suggest that the system/environment and system/system relations cannot be understood adequately within the parameters of sociological systems theory; this is just an aspect of the theory that still awaits a more convincing (less vague) solution, both theoretically and empirically.

Other blind spots might be identified as well. In continuation of what has just been touched upon *intensity* constitutes a blind spot in Luhmann's emphasis on binary logics. For Luhmann, it is always either–or (system/environment, government/opposition, payment/non-payment, etc.), and only very rarely a matter of more or less. Moreover, Luhmann is almost silent on the social role of *affect*. Recently, an entire 'affective turn' (e.g. Clough and Halley 2007) has been proclaimed within social theory, which studies the social role of affect, including among many other things how affect is engineered in the economy when products are designed so as to attach customers affectively to goods. One of the key points in this body of literature is that affect is not simply a personal phenomenon, but rather a social event. Although occasional remarks on emotions and affect can be found in Luhmann's work, Luc Ciompi

(2004) is correct in arguing that Luhmann offers no real place for affect in his sociology. Or to be more precise, Luhmann does consider affect and emotions, but conceives of them as merely 'pre-social', individual and consciousness-specific, and not as distinctively social phenomena. So Luhmann is blind to the genuinely *social* character of affect (Staubmann 2004). Finally, *materiality* might be said to constitute a blind spot in Luhmann's work. Due to his definition of sociality as communication only, Luhmann ignores how materiality (somewhat similar to spatiality) works to condition communication.

One might ask what implications these blind spots have. Two main options are available. *Either* one can endorse a Luhmannian framework to study those issues for which it is most apt (e.g. applying functionalism, second-order observation and functional differentiation where it makes sense) and turn to other sociologists for those issues where it is less suitable (space, affect, materiality, etc.). This would amount to a kind of specialisation argument: Luhmann is good for this, whereas Latour, Habermas, etc. are good for that. *Or* one can take seriously the blind spots in Luhmann's theory and try to deal with them internally, i.e. on basis of the propositions of systems theory. This option would amount to an accommodation of the identified weaknesses with the aim of improving the theoretical edifice that Luhmann has put forward. As I will argue in the concluding remarks below, the latter option is, in my view, the one most in line with Luhmann's way of working.

## IN THE FOOTSTEPS OF LUHMANN

Arguably, Luhmann's central legacy is not merely to be found in his specific analyses or in his conceptual apparatus. It might consist in his approach to theorising. Luhmann's work is characterised by an exceptional eclecticism where ideas and conceptual building blocks from various branches of sociology, philosophy, cybernetics, biology, etc. are picked out and incorporated into the theoretical architecture insofar as Luhmann considers them useful for his own endeavours (see also King and Thornhill 2003: 204–6). Only the distinction between system and environment, the foundation for his work, was sacred to him. Every other part is open for refinement and modification (although, of course, Luhmann did commit himself to specific positions throughout his career), and it matters little to him if this modification means incorporating ideas from immediately incommensurable theoretical traditions (e.g. Parsons, Maturana, Derrida).

Eclecticism comes at a price since it might lump together elements that do not fit. However, rather than debunking Luhmann's eclecticism

I think it should be commended, for it bears witness to an exceptionally open-minded way of working sociologically, which in Luhmann's case produced immense theoretical creativity and numerous thought-provoking ideas. To continue in the footsteps of Luhmann would therefore entail accepting the invitation to productive eclecticism that is at the heart of his work. More practically, this means that, although Luhmann developed a grand sociological theory, his approach to theorising suggests that working with systems theory is an open invitation to continuously developing it further by combining it with new theoretical bits and pieces. So rather than treating his systems theory dogmatically as a fixed, mummified entity, which should be preserved as it was left, it would be in Luhmann's own spirit to continue the receptive theoretical elaborations so as to enhance the sociological imagination.

# Notes

## 1 INTRODUCTION

1 In an editorial comment on the posthumously published version of the early text, André Kieserling wrongly remarks that the text was prepared in 1969 for one of Luhmann's first seminars in Bielefeld (Kieserling 2008: 94). I am grateful to Dirk Baecker for drawing my attention to this inaccuracy and, more generally, for clarifying this early step in Luhmann's career.

2 As Luhmann put it in an ironic formulation that played on the vocabulary of Habermas, '[s]ystems theory has emancipated itself from reason and domination' (1971b: 401).

3 This followed nicely from his functionalist method, according to which there is no true relation between a problem and its solution. As will be further examined in Chapters 4 and 5, the rejection of one true perspective on the social world is also a consequence of the differentiation of society into a multiplicity of self-referential systems.

4 The reception of Luhmann's work outside the field of sociology has been examined in detail in de Berg and Schmidt (2000).

## 2 SOCIAL SYSTEMS

1  Luhmann insists that his considerations on social systems 'do not deny that human beings exist, and they also do not deny the stark differences in living conditions in the different regions of the earth. *They only abstain from inferring from these facts a criterion for the definition of society*' (1997a: 35; Luhmann in Moeller 2006: 238–9, italics added).

2  At least not in the Luhmannian conception. Earlier notions of systems referred to the existence of a whole, itself composed of its parts. The advantage of the system/environment distinction over the whole/parts distinction lies in its ability to account at once for internal dynamics and for the relation to the system's outside. For a discussion of systems as a whole/parts construction, see Luhmann (1995g: 5–8).

3  The notions of ego and alter will be addressed below when I discuss Luhmann's understanding of communication.

4  He emphasises this in the light of suggestions that autopoiesis should be seen as an evolutionary achievement where autopoiesis is a matter of degree (e.g. Teubner 1993: 27).

5  In an interesting deconstructive reading of Luhmann's work, Andreas Philippopoulos-Mihalopoulos has argued that even within systems theory the main attention should lie with the environment (see Philippopoulos-Mihalopoulos 2010).

6  Figure 1 above lists main three kinds of social systems, namely interactions, organisations and societies. I will come back to this differentiation in Chapter 4.

7  According to Luhmann, 'the concepts of ego and alter (alter ego) do not stand for roles, persons, or systems, but for special horizons that collect and bind together meaningful references' (1995g: 80–1). Although ego and alter thus refer to 'interpretative possibilities' (1995g: 80), Luhmann's own examples typically treat ego and alter as either persons or systems.

8  For a penetrating analysis of this communicative reliance on action, see Stäheli (2000b). Stäheli argues that Luhmann's re-inscription of action into his theory of communication is not only unnecessary; more importantly, it diminishes the radicalism of Luhmann's theoretical proposal to base sociology on a strictly communication-theoretical edifice.

9  Luhmann comments on his inspiration and difference from Husserl's phenomenology in Luhmann (1986; 1996).

10  A similar point has recently been advanced by the German philosopher Peter Sloterdijk, who has great respect for Luhmann's work

(for a discussion of Sloterdijk and Luhmann, see Borch 2008). Sloterdijk has proposed a grand theory that describes modern society as foam, i.e. a complex composition of minor bubbles. According to Sloterdijk, one of the advantages of the notion of foam is that it is likely to resist political and powerful embracement and appropriation (Sloterdijk 2004: 866). What politician would demand more foam or new bubbles!

11  It should be noted that in his earliest writings, Luhmann did not promote an antihumanist programme. Quite the contrary, as Schimank (1996: 137) observes, he actually subscribed to an anthropological position which elevated the human being to the reference point of his sociological analysis; see in particular Luhmann (1970: 131, n. 9).

12  It is important to note that Luhmann talks of a society's *primary* mode of differentiation. It is perfectly possible in a modern functionally differentiated society to find elements of segmentary or hierarchical differentiation. The mafia, for example, embodies a segmentary differentiation within an otherwise functionally differentiated society (see Luhmann 1995d: 251–8).

## 3  OBSERVING SYSTEMS

1  For a discussion of Luhmann's reliance on Spencer-Brown, see Baecker (1993), Luhmann (1988d; 1999a) as well as Borch (2000) on which the following is partly based.

2  This, states Luhmann, marks the key difference between observations and perceptions. The latter are merely 'unformed distinctions', i.e. they register something, but not on the basis of a two-sided distinction (Luhmann 2000a: 28). However, perceptions may form the backdrop to observations; they can trigger the introduction of a distinction whose one side is indicated.

3  One might see a parallel here to Erving Goffman's *Frame Analysis* (see Borch 2000: 110). The problem Goffman sets out to analyse in this book is how people who interact deal with the fundamental question they recurrently face, namely '[w]hat is it that's going on here?' (Goffman 1974: 8). According to Goffman, this question can only be answered by taking into account the frame in which a particular situation is embedded. In order to act appropriately in a specific situation, one has to know the context of the distinctions that are applied. If the frame is changed, then the meaning of the distinctions change accordingly (which Goffman terms 'keying', see 1974: 43–5). Combining Goffman and Luhmann it may be

argued that every distinction has its own frame. Usually, people are aware of the frame which is currently activated. So adequate frame analysis is the rule, and misinterpretations might be sanctioned.

4  The transition from first to second-order observation marks the limits to *Laws of Form*. Spencer-Brown's treatise can be seen as a formalisation of first-order observations, i.e. of how a first-order observer draws distinctions, while recognising that other and higher levels exist, namely re-entered forms (Esposito 1993: 101). However, *Laws of Form* does not provide a formalisation of such higher levels. According to Elena Esposito, a formalisation of second-order observation requires a third (non-imaginary) value beyond marked and unmarked state (Esposito 1991: 54). The German logician Gotthard Günther, whom Luhmann often refers to in the discussions of such logical questions, has attempted to develop a many-valued logic which might be used to formalise second-order observations (for a discussion of Günther's work, see Klagenfurt 1995). Luhmann does not believe that Günther succeeded in this attempt and therefore mainly credits him for formulating the right problem (the need to go beyond two values) rather than for finding a proper solution to it.

5  He explicitly discusses third-order observation on a few occasions (e.g. 2000a: 61).

6  On the relation between Luhmann and Tarde, see Borch (2005c).

7  Many scholars working in the footsteps of Luhmann have pursued this discussion of how to relate systems theory and Derrida's decon-struction, see e.g. Philippopoulos-Mihalopoulos (2010), Rasch (2000), Stäheli (2000a) and Teubner (2001).

## 4  THE FUNCTIONAL DIFFERENTIATION OF MODERN SOCIETY

1  In some of his last work, Luhmann (1997a: 847 ff.) suggests that protest movements (for example, Greenpeace) might constitute an independent kind of system alongside the division into interaction, organisation and society. This option will not be discussed below.

2  This is only a rough approximation, though, as the key notion of social systems, communication, crisscrosses usual separations between such levels. The triple selection of information, utterance and understanding that constitutes communication is neither a micro, nor a meso, nor a macro phenomenon. Communication activates all these levels at once and cannot be reduced to any of them; it simply evades such a separation.

3   Luhmann is very explicit on the inspiration from Goffman and even argues that the latter's work contains proximities to systems theory (Luhmann 1975b: 34, n. 11).

4   For a full-fledged systems-theoretical analysis of interactions, see Kieserling (1999), though.

5   For analyses of Luhmann's notion of organisations, see Bakken and Hernes (2003), Seidl and Becker (2006).

6   For example, some scholars have argued for seeing sport as an independent function system (Bette 1999; Stichweh 1990), just as a function system of care and help has been identified (Baecker 1994).

7   In line with Luhmann's interest in paradoxes and de-paradoxification, he emphasises that the ongoing use of binary codes enacts a practical de-paradoxification of the underlying paradox which, he claims, characterises any code (e.g. 1989a: 39). This paradox becomes visible when the code is applied on itself. For example, is the distinction between true and false itself true? Is it legal to distinguish between legal and illegal (the legal system's code), etc? The function system unfolds (read: ignores) this paradox when it uses the code in its daily operations, and does not turn the code on itself.

8   Luhmann argues that no independent function system of moral has evolved. Moral constitutes a specific form of communication, though, which is concerned with attributing esteem or contempt to persons. This moral communication can be applied to any field. For example, politicians might be seen as acting in an immoral way, hence attracting contempt rather than esteem. Similarly, scientific work that requires animal testing might be observed as immoral, producing contempt for the particular scientists. It is because of this non-specialised applicability of moral communication that no separate function system of moral has developed, says Luhmann (see 2008c). Still, and this is the crucial point for now, in spite of the fact that any field can be subjected to moral communication, this does not mean that the various function systems' binary codes correspond to a moral coding.

9   This is one of the key points separating Luhmann's theory from what Parsons suggested. Parsons also developed a theory of symbolically generalised media, but he claimed that system differentiation preceded the development of the respective media. The problem with that argument is, in Luhmann's eyes, that this makes Parsons' theory too empirically insensitive. In Parsons, the media are mere deductions of the four subsystems that Parsons identified. According to Luhmann's theory, by contrast, the number of media is an

empirical question which cannot be deduced theoretically (see Luhmann 1976: 515).

10   The exception is values which did not develop into a binary code and subsequently into a distinct function system. This is also the reason why Luhmann hesitates to describe values as a symbolically generalised medium on par with the other media (1997a: 340).

11   The notions of the power-holder and the power-subject are taken from the English translation of Luhmann's book on power (e.g. 1979: 116) and tend to conceal that Luhmann's rejects to understand power as something that can be possessed (see Chapter 6).

12   Readers, who are interested in more thorough discussions of Luhmann's sociology of law, may be referred to the excellent analyses offered by King and Thornhill (2003), Nobles and Schiff (2004), Philippopoulos-Mihalopoulos (2010) and Teubner (1993).

13   Luhmann's most important discussion of the economic system is put forward in *Die Wirtschaft der Gesellschaft* (1988b). This book is not available in full English translation, although a few extracts have appeared in English, see Luhmann (1982b; 1997b). For discussions and illustrations of how systems theory can contribute to economic sociology, see Dirk Baecker (1991) and Jens Beckert (2002).

14   For an extensive discussion of the relation between Luhmann and Marx, see Pahl (2008).

15   While Luhmann explicitly recognises how his theory of functional differentiation has a Weberian legacy (e.g. 1987b: 19), he is generally very critical of any comparisons between his and Weber's work. In one interview, Luhmann states that 'I see (almost) no relation between my theoretical views and those of Max Weber' (Sciulli 1994: 44).

16   A different approach to integration will be discussed in Chapter 5 when I examine inclusion and exclusion.

## 5  CONSEQUENCES OF FUNCTIONAL DIFFERENTIATION

1   However, says Luhmann, the various function systems share an increasing focus on second-order observation. Thus, the political system observes the world in terms of how it will be observed by public opinion; artists make artworks with a view to how they will be observed by spectators, etc. (Luhmann 1997a: 766–7).

2   Due to this neglect Luhmann suggests that symbolically generalised media of communication might also be seen as *diabolic media*; they make certain things relevant but exclude all others (see 1988b: 245).

## 6 POWER AND POLITICS

1 King and Thornhill note that Luhmann also observes a welfare state de-differentiation on level of the internal differentiation of the political system. Due to the increase in regulatory burdens that the welfare state brings about, Luhmann's analysis suggests, '[t]he welfare state erodes the functional differentiations at the heart of the democratic political system, and it tends to fuse administration and politics together in one prerogative unit, thus eliminating the counterweights, checks and balances installed through their separation' (King and Thornhill 2003: 81).

2 The following sections draw on Borch (2005b), which presents an extensive discussion of Luhmann's theory of power.

# References

Agamben, G. (1998) *Homo Sacer: Sovereign Power and Bare Life*, trans. Daniel Heller-Roazen, Stanford, California: Stanford University Press.

Alexander, J. C. and Colomy, P. (1990) *Differentiation Theory and Social Change: Comparative and Historical Perspectives*, New York: Columbia University Press.

Andersen, N. Å. (2003) *Discursive analytical strategies: Understanding Foucault, Koselleck, Laclau, Luhmann*, Bristol: The Policy Press.

Andersen, N. Å. (2008) *Partnerships: Machines of Possibility*, Bristol: The Policy Press.

Andersen, N. Å. (2009) *Power at play: The relationships between play, work and governance*, Basingstoke: Palgrave Macmillan.

Anz, T. (2009) 'Niklas Luhmanns rätselhaftes Gastspiel im Zentrum Kritischer Theorie: Über eine abgebrochene Spurensuche – mit einer Nachbemerkung zu Jürgen Habermas' Stil wissenschaftlicher Kommunikation', *literaturkritik.de* 6(June) www.literaturkritik.de/public/rezension.php?rez_id=13166 (consulted May 2010).

Arnoldi, J. (2009) *Risk: An Introduction*, Cambridge: Polity Press.

Baecker, D. (1991) *Womit handeln Banken? Eine Untersuchung zur Risikoverarbeitung in der Wirtschaft, with an Introduction by Niklas Luhmann*, Frankfurt am Main: Suhrkamp.

Baecker, D. (1993) 'Im Tunnel', pp. 12–37 in D. Baecker (ed.) *Kalkül der Form*, Frankfurt am Main: Suhrkamp.

Baecker, D. (1994) 'Soziale Hilfe als Funktionssystem der Gesellschaft', *Zeitschrift für Soziologie* 23(2): 91–110.

Baecker, D. (1999a) 'Introduction', pp. 1–14 in D. Baecker (ed.) *Problems of Form*, trans. Michael Irmscher, with Leah Edwards, Stanford, California: Stanford University Press.

Baecker, D. (1999b) 'When etwas der Fall ist, steckt auch etwas dahinter', pp. 35–48 in R. Stichweh (ed.) *Niklas Luhmann: Wirkungen eines Theoretikers: Gedenkcolloquium der Universität Bielefeld am 8. Dezember 1998*, Bielefeld: Transcript.

Bakken, T. and Hernes, T. (eds) (2003) *Autopoietic Organization Theory: Drawing on Niklas Luhmann's Social Systems Perspective*. Olso: Abstrakt.

Balke, F. (2002) 'Tristes Tropiques: Systems Theory and the Literary Scene', *Soziale Systeme* 8(1): 27–37.

Bateson, G. (2000) *Steps to an Ecology of Mind*, Chicago, Illinois and London: University of Chicago Press.

Bauman, Z. (1997) *Postmodernity and its Discontents*, Cambridge: Polity Press.

Bauman, Z. (2002) *Society under Siege*, Cambridge: Polity Press.

Bauman, Z. (2004) *Wasted Lives: Modernity and its Outcasts*, Cambridge: Polity Press.

Beck, U. (1992) *Risk Society: Towards a New Modernity*, trans. Mark Ritter, London: Sage.

Beck, U. (1994) 'The Reinvention of Politics: Towards a Theory of Reflexive Modernization', pp. 1–55 in U. Beck, Giddens, A. and Lash, S. (eds) *Reflexive Modernization: Politics, Tradition and Aesthetics in the Modern Social Order*, Cambridge: Polity Press.

Beck, U. (1995) *Ecological Politics in an Age of Risk*, trans. Amos Weisz, Cambridge: Polity Press.

Beckert, J. (2002) *Beyond the Market: The Social Foundations of Economic Efficiency*, trans. Barbara Harshav, Princeton, New Jersey and Oxford: Princeton University Press.

Berger, P. L. and Luckmann, T. (1966) *The Social Construction of Reality: A Treatise in the Sociology of Knowledge*, London: Penguin Books.

Bette, K.-H. (1999) *Systemtheorie und Sport*, Frankfurt am Main: Suhrkamp.

Borch, C. (2000) 'Former, der kommer i form—om Luhmann og Spencer–Brown', *Distinktion* 1: 105–22.

Borch, C. (2005a) *Kriminalitet og magt. Kriminalitetsopfattelser i det 20. århundrede*, Copenhagen: Forlaget politisk revy.

Borch, C. (2005b) 'Systemic Power: Luhmann, Foucault, and Analytics of Power', *Acta Sociologica* 48(2): 155–67.

Borch, C. (2005c) 'Urban Imitations: Tarde's Sociology Revisited', *Theory, Culture & Society* 22(3): 81–100.

Borch, C. (2008) 'Foam architecture: managing co-isolated associations', *Economy and Society* 37(4): 548–71.

Bourdieu, P. (1986) 'The Forms of Capital', pp. 241–258 in J. G. Richardson (ed.) *Handbook of Theory and Research for the Sociology of Education*, New York: Greenwood Press.

Castells, M. (1996) *The Rise of the Network Society*, Oxford: Blackwell.

Ciompi, L. (2004) 'Ein blinder Fleck bei Niklas Luhmann? Soziale Wirkungen von Emotionen aus Sicht der fraktalen Affektlogik', *Soziale Systeme* 10(1): 21–49.

Clough, P. T. and Halley, J. (eds) (2007) *The Affective Turn: Theorizing the Social*. Durham, North Carolina and London: Duke University Press.

de Berg, H. and Schmidt, J. (2000) *Rezeption und Reflexion: Zur Resonanz der Systemtheorie Niklas Luhmanns außerhalb der Soziologie*, Frankfurt am Main: Suhrkamp.

Durkheim, E. (1964) *The Division of Labor In Society*, trans. George Simpson, New York: The Free Press of Glencoe.

Esposito, E. (1991) 'Paradoxien als Unterscheidungen von Unterscheidungen', pp. 35–57 in H. U. Gumbrecht and Pfeiffer, K. L. (eds) *Paradoxien, Dissonanzen, Zusammenbrüche: Situationen offener Epistemologie*, Frankfurt am Main: Suhrkamp.

Esposito, E. (1993) 'Ein zweiwertiger nicht-selbständiger Kalkül', pp. 96–111 in D. Baecker (ed.) *Kalkül der Form*, Frankfurt am Main: Suhrkamp.

Filippov, A. (2000) 'Wo befinden sich Systeme? Ein blinder Fleck der Systemtheorie', pp. 381–410 in P.-U. Merz-Benz and Wagner, G. (eds) *Die Logik der Systeme. Zur Kritik der systemtheoretischen Soziologie Niklas Luhmanns*, Constance: UVK.

Foucault, M. (1977) *Discipline and Punish: The Birth of the Prison*, London: Penguin.

Foucault, M. (1982) 'The Subject and Power', pp. 208–26 in H. L. Dreyfus and Rabinow, P. *Michel Foucault: Beyond Structuralism and Hermeneutics*, Chicago, Illinois: University of Chicago Press.

Foucault, M. (1990) *The History of Sexuality, Vol. 1: An Introduction*, trans. Robert Hurley, New York: Vintage Books.

Foucault, M. (1997) 'Polemics, Politics, and Problematizations: An Interview with Michel Foucault', pp. 111–19 in *Ethics: Subjectivity and Truth. The Essential Works of Michel Foucault 1954–1984, Vol. 1*, ed. Paul Rabinow, New York: The Free Press.

Foucault, M. (2003) *"Society Must Be Defended": Lectures at the Collegè de France, 1975–1976*, New York: Picador.

Girard, R. (1977) *Violence and the Sacred*, trans. Patrick Gregory, Baltimore, Maryland and London: The Johns Hopkins University Press.

Göbel, M. and Schmidt, J. (1998) 'Inklusion/Exklusion: Karriere, Probleme und Differenzierungen eines systemtheoretischen Begriffspaar', *Soziale Systeme* 4(1): 87–117.

Goffman, E. (1963) *Stigma: Notes on the Management of Spoiled Identity*, Englewood Cliffs, New Jersey: Prentice-Hall.

Goffman, E. (1974) *Frame Analysis: An Essay on the Organization of Experience*, New York: Harper & Row.

Granovetter, M. (1985) 'Economic Action and Social Structure: The Problem of Embeddedness', *American Journal of Sociology* 91(3): 481–510.

Günther, G. (1979) 'Life as Poly-Contexturality', pp. 283–306 in *Beiträge zur Grundlegung einer operationsfähigen Dialektik, Vol. 2*, Hamburg: Felix Meiner Verlag.

Habermas, J. (1971) 'Theorie der Gesellschaft order Sozialtechnologie? Eine Auseinandersetzung mit Niklas Luhmann', pp. 142–290 in J. Habermas and Luhmann, N. *Theorie der Gesellschaft oder Sozialtechnologie. Was leistet die Systemforschung?*, Frankfurt am Main: Suhrkamp.

Habermas, J. (1984) *The Theory of Communicative Action, Vol. 1: Reason and the Rationalization of Society*, trans. Thomas McCarthy, Boston, Massachusetts: Beacon Press.

Habermas, J. (1987) '*Excursus on Luhmann's Appropriation of the Philosophy of the Subject through Systems Theory*', pp. 368–85 in *The Philosophical Discourse of Modernity: Twelve Lectures*, trans. Frederick Lawrence, Cambridge: Polity Press.

Højlund, H. (2009) 'Hybrid inclusion: the new consumerism of Danish welfare services', *Journal of European Social Policy* 19(5): 421–31.

Horster, D. (1997) *Niklas Luhmann*, Munich: Verlag C. H. Beck.

Jokisch, R. (1996) *Logik der Distinktionen: Zur Protologik einer Theorie der Gesellschaft*, Opladen: Westdeutscher Verlag.

Kauffman, L. (1987) 'Self-reference and recursive forms', *Journal of Social and Biological Structures* 10(1): 53–72.

Kieserling, A. (1999) *Kommunikation unter Anwesenden: Studien über Interaktionssysteme*, Frankfurt am Main: Suhrkamp.

Kieserling, A. (2008) 'Editorische Notiz', pp. 93–5 in N. Luhmann *Liebe: Eine Übung*, Frankfurt am Main: Suhrkamp.

King, M. and Thornhill, C. (2003) *Niklas Luhmann's Theory of Politics and Law*, Houndmills, Basingstoke: Palgrave Macmillan.

Klagenfurt, K. (1995) *Technologische Zivilisation und transklassische Logik. Eine Einführung in die Technikphilosophie Gotthard Günthers*, Frankfurt am Main: Suhrkamp.

Kluge, A. (2009) *Das Labyrinth der zärtlichen Kraft. 166 Liebesgeschichten*, Frankfurt am Main: Suhrkamp.

Kneer, G. (2004) 'Differenzierung bei Luhmann und Bourdieu. Ein Theorienvergleich', pp. 25–56 in A. Nassehi and Nollmann, G. (eds) *Bourdieu und Luhmann. Ein Theorienvergleich*, Frankfurt am Main: Suhrkamp.

Kneer, G. and Nassehi, A. (1993) *Niklas Luhmanns Theorie sozialer Systeme. Eine Einführung*, Munich: Wilhelm Fink Verlag.

Knodt, E. M. (1995) 'Foreword', pp. ix–xxxvi in N. Luhmann *Social Systems*, Stanford, California: Stanford University Press.

Latour, B. (1993) *We Have Never Been Modern*, trans. Catherine Porter, Cambridge, Massachusetts: Harvard University Press.

Latour, B. (2004) *Politics of Nature: How to Bring the Sciences into Democracy*, trans. Catherine Porter, Cambridge, Massachusetts: Harvard University Press.

Latour, B. (2005) *Reassembling the Social: An Introduction to Actor-Network-Theory*, Oxford: Oxford University Press.

Lemke, T. (1997) *Eine Kritik der politischen Vernunft. Foucaults Analyse der modernen Gouvernementalität*, Hamburg und Berlin: Argument.

Luhmann, N. (1962) 'Funktion und Kausalität', *Kölner Zeitschrift für Soziologie und Sozialpsychologie* 14: 617–44.

Luhmann, N. (1964) 'Funktionale Methode und Systemtheorie', *Soziale Welt* 15: 1–25.

Luhmann, N. (1967a) 'Soziologie als Theorie sozialer Systeme', *Kölner Zeitschrift für Soziologie und Sozialpsychologie* 19: 615–44.

Luhmann, N. (1967b) 'Soziologische Aufklärung', *Soziale Welt* 18: 97–123.

Luhmann, N. (1969) 'Klassische Theorie der Macht: Kritik ihrer Prämissen', *Zeitschrift für Politik* 16: 149–70.

Luhmann, N. (1970) 'Soziologie als Theorie sozialer Systeme', pp. 113–36 in *Soziologische Aufklärung, Vol. 1: Aufsätze zur Theorie sozialer Systeme*, Opladen: Westdeutscher Verlag.

Luhmann, N. (1971a) 'Sinn als Grundbegriff der Soziologie', pp. 25–100 in J. Habermas and N. Luhmann, *Theorie der Gesellschaft oder Sozialtechnologie. Was leistet die Systemforschung?*, Frankfurt am Main: Suhrkamp.

Luhmann, N. (1971b) 'Systemtheoretische Argumentationen. Eine Entgegnung auf Jürgen Habermas', pp. 291–405 in J. Habermas and Luhmann, N. *Theorie der Gesellschaft oder Sozialtechnologie. Was leistet die Systemforschung?*, Frankfurt am Main: Suhrkamp.

Luhmann, N. (1975a) 'Interaktion, Organisation, Gesellschaft: Anwendungen der Systemtheorie', pp. 5–20 in *Soziologische Aufklärung, Vol. 2: Aufsätze zur Theorie der Gesellschaft*, Opladen: Westdeutscher Verlag.

Luhmann, N. (1975b) 'Einfache Sozialsysteme', pp. 21–38 in *Soziologische Aufklärung, Vol. 2: Aufsätze zur Theorie der Gesellschaft*, Opladen: Westdeutscher Verlag.

Luhmann, N. (1976) 'Generalized Media and the Problem of Contingency', pp. 507–32 in J. J. Loubser et al. (eds) *Explorations in General Theory in Social Science: Essays in Honor of Talcott Parsons, Vol. 2.*, New York: The Free Press.

Luhmann, N. (1979) *Trust and Power: Two works*, with an Introduction by Gianfranco Poggi, Chichester and New York: John Wiley & Sons.

Luhmann, N. (1981a) *Gesellschaftsstruktur und Semantik. Studien zur Wissenssoziologie der modernen Gesellschaft, Vol. 2*, Frankfurt am Main: Suhrkamp.

Luhmann, N. (1981b) *Politische Theorie im Wohlfahrtsstaat*, Munich: Günter Olzog Verlag.

Luhmann, N. (1982a) 'Durkheim on Morality and the Division of Labor', pp. 3–19 in *The Differentiation of Society*, trans. Stephen Holmes and Charles Larmore, New York: Columbia University Press.

Luhmann, N. (1982b) 'The Economy as a Social System', pp. 190–225 in *The Differentiation of Society*, trans. Stephen Holmes and Charles Larmore, New York: Columbia University Press.

Luhmann, N. (1982c) 'The Differentiation of Society', pp. 229–54 in *The Differentiation of Society*, trans. Stephen Holmes and Charles Larmore, New York: Columbia University Press.

Luhmann, N. (1986) 'Die Lebenswelt – nach Rücksprache mit Phänomenologen', *Archiv für Rechts- und Sozialphilosophie* 76(2): 176–94.

Luhmann, N. (1987a) *Archimedes und wir. Interviews*, ed. Dirk Baecker and Georg Stanitzek, Berlin: Merve Verlag.

Luhmann, N. (1987b) ' "Distinctions directrices". Über Codierung von Semantiken und Systemen', pp. 13–31 in *Soziologische Aufklärung, Vol. 4: Beiträge zur funktionalen Differenzierung der Gesellschaft*, Opladen: Westdeutscher Verlag.

Luhmann, N. (1987c) *Rechtssoziologie*, 3rd edn, Opladen: Westdeutscher Verlag.

Luhmann, N. (1988a) 'Die "Macht der Verhältnisse" und die Macht der Politik', pp. 43–51 in H. Schneider (ed.) *Macht und Ohnmacht*, Vienna: St. Pölten.

Luhmann, N. (1988b) *Die Wirtschaft der Gesellschaft*, Frankfurt am Main: Suhrkamp.

Luhmann, N. (1988c) *Erkenntnis als Konstruktion*, Berne: Benteli Verlag.

Luhmann, N. (1988d) 'Frauen, Männer und George Spencer Brown', *Zeitschrift für Soziologie* 17(1): 47–71.

Luhmann, N. (1988e) 'The Third Question: The Creative Use of Paradoxes in Law and Legal History', *Journal of Law and Society* 15(2): 153–65.

Luhmann, N. (1989a) *Ecological Communication*, trans. and introduced by John Bednarz Jr, Cambridge: Polity Press.

Luhmann, N. (1989b) 'Individuum, Individualität, Individualismus', pp. 149–258 in *Gesellschaftsstruktur und Semantik, Vol. 3*, Frankfurt am Main: Suhrkamp.

Luhmann, N. (1990a) *Die Wissenschaft der Gesellschaft*, Frankfurt am Main: Suhrkamp.

Luhmann, N. (1990b) 'The Future of Democracy', *Thesis Eleven* 26: 46–53.

Luhmann, N. (1990c) 'The Paradox of System Differentiation and the Evolution of Society', pp. 409–40 in J. C. Alexander and Colomy, P. (eds) *Differentiation Theory and Social Change: Comparative and Historical Perspectives*, New York: Columbia University Press.

Luhmann, N. (1990d) *Political Theory in the Welfare State*, Berlin and New York: De Gruyter.

Luhmann, N. (1990e) 'State and Politics: Towards a Semantics of the Self-Description of Political Systems', pp. 117–154 in *Political Theory in the Welfare State*, trans. and introduced by John Bednarz, Jr, Berlin and New York: Walter de Gruyter.

Luhmann, N. (1990f) 'Societal Foundations of Power: Increase and Distribution', pp. 155–165 in *Political Theory in the Welfare State*, trans.

and introduced by John Bednarz, Jr, Berlin and New York: Walter de Gruyter.

Luhmann, N. (1990g) 'Risiko und Gefahr', pp. 131–69 in *Soziologische Aufklärung, Vol. 5: Konstruktivistische Perspektiven*, Opladen: Westdeutscher Verlag.

Luhmann, N. (1990h) 'Der medizinische Code', pp. 183–95 in *Soziologische Aufklärung, Vol. 5: Konstruktivistische Perspektiven*, Opladen: Westdeutscher Verlag.

Luhmann, N. (1990i) 'Sozialsystem Familie', pp. 196–217 in *Soziologische Aufklärung, Vol. 5: Konstruktivistische Perspektiven*, Opladen: Westdeutscher Verlag.

Luhmann, N. (1990j) 'Sthenographie', pp. 119–37 in N. Luhmann et al. *Beobachter. Konvergenz der Erkenntnistheorien?*, Munich: Wilhelm Fink Verlag.

Luhmann, N. (1990k) 'Meaning as Sociology's Basic Concept', pp. 21–79 in *Essays on Self-Reference*, New York: Columbia University Press.

Luhmann, N. (1990l) 'The Improbability of Communication', pp. 86–98 in *Essays on Self-Reference*, New York: Columbia University Press.

Luhmann, N. (1990m) 'The World Society as a Social System', pp. 175–90 in *Essays on Self-Reference*, New York: Columbia University Press.

Luhmann, N. (1990n) 'The Medium of Art', pp. 215–26 in *Essays on Self-Reference*, New York: Columbia University Press.

Luhmann, N. (1991) 'Am Ende der kritischen Soziologie', *Zeitschrift für Soziologie* 20(2): 147–52.

Luhmann, N. (1992a) 'Kommunikation mit Zettelkästen: Ein Erfahrungsbericht', pp. 53–61 in *Universität als Milieu. Kleine Schriften*, ed. André Kieserling, Bielefeld: Haux.

Luhmann, N. (1992b) 'Operational Closure and Structural Coupling: The Differentiation of the Legal System', *Cardozo Law Review* 13: 1419–41.

Luhmann, N. (1993a) *Das Recht der Gesellschaft*, Frankfurt am Main: Suhrkamp.

Luhmann, N. (1993b) 'Deconstruction as Second-Order Observing', *New Literary History* 24: 763–82.

Luhmann, N. (1993c) 'Observing Re-entries', *Graduate Faculty Philosophy Journal* 16(2): 485–98.

Luhmann, N. (1993d) *Risk: A Sociological Theory*, trans. Rhodes Barrett, Berlin and New York: Walter de Gruyter.

Luhmann, N. (1994a) 'Die Tücke des Subjekts und die Frage nach den Menschen', pp. 40–56 in P. Fuchs and Göbel, A. (eds) *Der Mensch – das Medium der Gesellschaft?*, Frankfurt am Main: Suhrkamp.

Luhmann, N. (1994b) 'The Idea of Unity in a Differentiated Society', paper presented at the XIIIth Sociological World Congress, Bielefeld, Germany (July).

Luhmann, N. (1994c) 'Politicians, Honesty and the Higher Amorality of Politics', *Theory, Culture & Society* 11(2): 25–36.

Luhmann, N. (1994d) ' "What Is the Case?" and "What Lies Behind It?" The Two Sociologies and The Theory of Society', *Sociological Theory* 12(2): 126–39.

Luhmann, N. (1995a) *Die Kunst der Gesellschaft*, Frankfurt am Main: Suhrkamp.

Luhmann, N. (1995b) 'Die gesellschaftliche Differenzierung und das Individuum', pp. 125–41 in *Soziologische Aufklärung 6. Die Soziologie und der Mensch*, Opladen: Westdeutscher Verlag.

Luhmann, N. (1995c) 'Das Kind als Medium der Erziehung', pp. 204–28 in *Soziologische Aufklärung 6. Die Soziologie und der Mensch*, Opladen: Westdeutscher Verlag.

Luhmann, N. (1995d) 'Inklusion und Exklusion', pp. 237–64 in *Soziologische Aufklärung 6. Die Soziologie und der Mensch*, Opladen: Westdeutscher Verlag.

Luhmann, N. (1995e) 'Kausalität im Süden', *Soziale Systeme* 1(1): 7–28.

Luhmann, N. (1995f) 'The Paradoxy of Observing Systems', *Cultural Critique* 31: 37–55.

Luhmann, N. (1995g) *Social Systems*, trans. John Bednarz, Jr., with Dirk Baecker, Stanford, California: Stanford University Press.

Luhmann, N. (1995h) 'Why Does Society Describe Itself as Postmodern?', *Cultural Critique* 30(Spring): 171–86.

Luhmann, N. (1996) *Die neuzeitlichen Wissenschaften und die Phänomenologie*, Vienna: Picus Verlag.

Luhmann, N. (1997a) *Die Gesellschaft der Gesellschaft*, Frankfurt am Main: Suhrkamp.

Luhmann, N. (1997b) 'Limits of Steering', *Theory, Culture & Society* 14(1): 41–57.

Luhmann, N. (1997c) 'Selbstreferentielle Systeme', pp. 69–79 in F. B. Simon (ed.) *Lebende Systeme: Wirklichkeitskonstruktionen in der systemischen Therapie*, Frankfurt am Main: Suhrkamp.

Luhmann, N. (1998a) *Love as Passion: The Codification of Intimacy*, trans. Jeremy Gaines and Doris L. Jones, Stanford, California: Stanford University Press.

Luhmann, N. (1998b) 'Modernity in Contemporary Society', pp. 1–21 in *Observations on Modernity*, trans. William Whobrey, Stanford, California: Stanford University Press.

Luhmann, N. (1998c) 'Contingency as Modern Society's Defining Attribute', pp. 44–62 in *Observations on Modernity*, trans. William Whobrey, Stanford, California: Stanford University Press.

Luhmann, N. (1999a) 'The Paradox of Form', pp. 15–26 in D. Baecker (ed.) *Problems of Form*, trans. Michael Irmscher with Leah Edwards, Stanford, California: Stanford University Press.

Luhmann, N. (1999b) 'Sign as Form', pp. 46–63 in D. Baecker (ed.) *Problems of Form*, trans. Michael Irmscher with Leah Edwards, Stanford, California: Stanford University Press.

Luhmann, N. (2000a) *Art as a Social System*, trans. Eva M. Knodt, Stanford, California: Stanford University Press.

Luhmann, N. (2000b) *Die Politik der Gesellschaft*, ed. André Kieserling, Frankfurt am Main: Suhrkamp.

Luhmann, N. (2000c) *Die Religion der Gesellschaft*, ed. André Kieserling, Frankfurt am Main: Suhrkamp.

Luhmann, N. (2000d) *Organisation und Entscheidung*, Opladen: Westdeutscher Verlag.

Luhmann, N. (2000e) *The Reality of the Mass Media*, trans. Kathleen Cross, Cambridge: Polity Press.

Luhmann, N. (2002a) *Einführung in die Systemtheorie*, ed. Dirk Baecker, Heidelberg: Carl-Auer-Systeme Verlag.

Luhmann, N. (2002b) *Das Erziehungssystem der Gesellschaft*, ed. Dieter Lenzen, Frankfurt am Main: Suhrkamp.

Luhmann, N. (2002c) 'Identity – What or How?, pp. 113–27 in *Theories of Distinction: Redescribing the Descriptions of Modernity*, ed. William Rasch, Stanford, California: Stanford University Press.

Luhmann, N. (2002d) 'The Cognitive Program of Constructivism and the Reality That Remains Unknown', pp. 128–52 in *Theories of Distinction: Redescribing the Descriptions of Modernity*, ed. William Rasch, Stanford, California: Stanford University Press.

Luhmann, N. (2002e) 'What Is Communication?', pp. 155–68 in *Theories of Distinction: Redescribing the Descriptions of Modernity*, ed. William Rasch, Stanford, California: Stanford University Press.

Luhmann, N. (2002f) 'How Can the Mind Participate in Communication?, pp. 169–84 in *Theories of Distinction: Redescribing the Descriptions of Modernity*, ed. William Rasch, Stanford, California: Stanford University Press.

Luhmann, N. (2002g) 'I See Something You Don't See', pp. 187–93 in *Theories of Distinction: Redescribing the Descriptions of Modernity*, ed. William Rasch, Stanford, California: Stanford University Press.

Luhmann, N. (2004) *Law as a Social System*, trans. Klaus A. Ziegert, Oxford: Oxford University Press.

Luhmann, N. (2006) 'System as Difference', *Organization* 13(1): 37–57.

Luhmann, N. (2008a) 'Beyond Barbarism', *Soziale Systeme* 14(1): 38–46.

Luhmann, N. (2008b) *Liebe: Eine Übung*, ed. André Kieserling, Frankfurt am Main: Suhrkamp.

Luhmann, N. (2008c) 'Soziologie der Moral', pp. 56–162 in *Die Moral der Gesellschaft,* ed. Detlef Horster, Frankfurt am Main: Suhrkamp.

Lyotard, J. F. (1984) *The Postmodern Condition: A Report on Knowledge*, Minneapolis: University of Minnesota Press.

Maturana, H. (1981) 'Autopoiesis', pp. 21–33 in M. Zeleny (ed.) *Autopoiesis: A Theory of Living Organization*, New York and Oxford: North Holland.

Maturana, H. (2002) 'Autopoiesis, Structural Coupling and Cognition: A history of these and other notions in the biology of cognition', *Cybernetics & Human Knowing* 9(3–4): 5–34.

Mingers, J. (2008) 'Can social systems be autopoietic? Assessing Luhmann's social theory', *Sociological Review* 50(2): 278–99.

Moeller, H.-G. (2006) *Luhmann Explained: From Souls to Systems*, Chicago and La Salle, Illinois: Open Court.

Mortensen, N. (2004) *Det paradoksale samfund. Undersøgelser af forholdet mellem individ og samfund*, Copenhagen: Hans Reitzels Forlag.

Nassehi, A. (2002) 'Exclusion Individuality or Individualization by Inclusion?', *Soziale Systeme* 8(1): 124–35.

Nassehi, A. and Nollmann, G. (eds) (2004) *Bourdieu und Luhmann. Ein Theorienvergleich*. Frankfurt am Main: Suhrkamp.

Nobles, R. and Schiff, D. (2004) 'Introduction', pp. 1–52 in N. Luhmann *Law as a Social System*, Oxford: Oxford University Press.

Pahl, H. (2008) *Das Geld in der modernen Wirtschaft. Marx und Luhmann im Vergleich*, Frankfurt am Main and New York: Campus Verlag.

Parsons, T. (1951) *The Social System*, London: Routledge and Kegan Paul.

Parsons, T. (1969) 'On the Concept of Political Power', pp. 352–404 in *Politics and Social Structure*, New York: The Free Press.

Parsons, T. and Smelser, N. J. (1956) *Economy and Society*, London: Routledge and Kegan Paul.

Philippopoulos-Mihalopoulos, A. (2008) 'On Absence: Society's Return to Barbarians', *Soziale Systeme* 14(1): 142–56.

Philippopoulos-Mihalopoulos, A. (2010) *Niklas Luhmann: Law, justice, society*, London and New York: Routledge.

Precht, R. D. (2009) *Liebe. Ein unordentliches Gefühl*, Munich: Goldmann Verlag.

Rasch, W. (2000) *Niklas Luhmann's Modernity: The Paradoxes of Differentiation*, Stanford, California: Stanford University Press.

Reese-Schäfer, W. (1992) *Luhmann zur Einführung*, Hamburg: Junius.

Rose, N. (1996) 'Governing "advanced" liberal democracies', pp. 37–64 in A. Barry, Osborne, T. and Rose, N. (eds) *Foucault and political reason: Liberalism, neo-liberalism and rationalities of government*, Chicago, Illinois and London: University of Chicago Press.

Schaff, A. (1962) *Introduction to Semantics,* trans. Olgierd Wojtasiewicz, Oxford: Pergamon Press.

Schimank, U. (1996) *Theorien gesellschaftlicher Differenzierung*, Opladen: Leske + Budrich.

Schulze, G. (1992) *Die Erlebnisgesellschaft: Kultursoziologie der Gegenwart*, Frankfurt am Main: Campus.

Sciulli, D. (1994) 'An Interview with Niklas Luhmann', *Theory, Culture & Society* 11(2): 37–68.

Seidl, D. and Becker, K. H. (2006) 'Organizations as Distinction Generating and Processing Systems: Niklas Luhmann's Contribution to Organization Studies', *Organization* 13(1): 9–35.

Simmel, G. (1989) 'Über sociale Differenzierung: Sociologische und psychologische Untersuchungen', pp. 109–295 in *Georg Simmel Gesamtausgabe, Vol. 2*, Frankfurt am Main: Suhrkamp.

Sloterdijk, P. (2004) *Sphären III. Schäume*, Frankfurt am Main: Suhrkamp.

Spencer-Brown, G. (1969) *Laws of Form*, London: George Allen and Unwin.

Stäheli, U. (2000a) *Sinnzusammenbrüche. Eine dekonstruktive Lektüre von Niklas Luhmanns Systemtheorie*, Weilerswist: Velbrück Wissenschaft.

Stäheli, U. (2000b) 'Writing Action: Double Contingency and Normalization', *Distinktion* 1: 39–47.

Staubmann, H. (2004) 'Der affektive Aufbau der sozialen Welt', *Soziale Systeme* 10(1): 140–58.

Stichweh, R. (1990) 'Sport – Ausdifferenzierung, Funktion, Code', *Sportwissenschaft* 20: 373–89.

Stichweh, R. (1998) 'Raum, Region und Stadt in der Systemtheorie', *Soziale Systeme* 4(2): 341–58.

Stichweh, R. (2002) 'Strangers, Inclusions, and Identities', *Soziale Systeme* 8(1): 101–09.

Tarde, G. (1962) *The Laws of Imitation*, Gloucester, Massachusetts: Peter Smith.

Teubner, G. (1993) *Law as an Autopoietic System*, trans. Anne Bankowska and Ruth Adler, Oxford: Blackwell.

Teubner, G. (2001) 'Economics of Gift – Positivity of Justice: The Mutual Paranoia of Jacques Derrida and Niklas Luhmann', *Theory, Culture & Society* 18(1): 29–47.

Thornhill, C. (2006) 'Niklas Luhmann: A Sociological Transformation of Political Legitimacy?', *Distinktion* 13: 33–53.

von Foerster, H. (1984a) *Observing Systems*, 2nd edn, Seaside, Caifornia: Intersystems Publications.

von Foerster, H. (1984b) 'On Constructing a Reality', pp. 288–309 in *Observing Systems*, 2nd edn, Seaside, California: Intersystems Publications.

von Foerster, H. (1992) 'Entdecken order Erfinden: Wie läßt sich Verstehen verstehen?', pp. 41–88 in E. von Glaserfeld et al. *Einführung in den Konstruktivismus*, Munich: Piper.

Weber, M. (1920) *Gesammelte Aufsätze zur Religionssoziologie, Vol. 1*, Tübingen: J.C.B. Mohr.

Weber, M. (1978) *Economy and Society: An Outline of Interpretive Sociology*, ed. Guenther Roth and Claus Wittic, Berkeley, Los Angeles and London: University of California Press.

# Index